All the

Wrong Places

Also by Philip Connors

Fire Season: Field Notes from a Wilderness Lookout

All the Wrong Places

A Life Lost and Found

PHILIP CONNORS

W. W. NORTON & COMPANY

New York · London

For information about permission to reproduce selections from this
book, write to Permissions, W. W. Norton & Company, Inc.,
500 Fifth Avenue, New York, NY 10110

For information about special discounts for bulk purchases,
please contact W. W. Norton Special Sales at
specialsales@wwnorton.com or 800-233-4830

Manufacturing by Courier Westford
Book design by Mary Austin Speaker
Production manager: Anna Oler

ISBN 978-0-393-08876-2

W. W. Norton & Company, Inc.
500 Fifth Avenue, New York, N.Y. 10110
www.wwnorton.com

W. W. Norton & Company Ltd.
Castle House, 75/76 Wells Street, London W1T 3QT

1 2 3 4 5 6 7 8 9 0

Author's Note

Some names and identifying details have been changed in an effort to protect the innocent and the guilty.

Portions of this book first appeared, in different form, in *n+1*, *Ninth Letter*, the *Dublin Review*, and *Lapham's Quarterly*, the editors of which are gratefully acknowledged; special thanks are due Keith Gessen, Brendan Barrington, and Elias Altman.

For M.J.

All the
Wrong Places

PART ONE

Up in the Air

A sense of obligation drew me to the Southwest that first time. My brother had recently proposed to his girlfriend, and although we weren't close—I'd seen him just once in the two years since he'd moved to New Mexico—meeting his fiancée before the week of their wedding seemed like the brotherly thing to do. With the celebration just a few months away, my January break at college offered the last best chance to get an introduction.

I reached Albuquerque in two long days of driving, only to find we were the same oddball brothers we'd always been, perhaps more so. He shook my hand in our aunt and uncle's driveway, pointy-toed boots on his feet, a ten-gallon hat on his head: playing cowboy, I thought, a little derisively. I'd arrived in my own borrowed costume, the garb of the campus outlaw, black combat boots and surplus East German Army pants, aggressive sideburns sculpted on my cheeks. If we hadn't been brothers and we'd passed in the street, one look would have soured me on him, and no doubt him on me.

My soon-to-be sister-in-law was a pale kid with hair dyed black and nails painted purple, a look that spoke of

3

rebellious instincts not at all in keeping with the vision I'd had of my brother's future wife. She was seventeen years old, the daughter of Dan's boss, an electrician who would soon make Dan foreman of his own crew. Emily would graduate from high school just weeks before the wedding. She showed an adoring deference toward Dan—a kind of puppyish infatuation in her eyes and in the tilt of her head— that I knew would one day fade, and I hoped it wouldn't curdle when it did, not least because she was the boss's daughter. She appeared inordinately curious about me, as if every word out of my mouth might contain a clue to parts of Dan's past and personality about which she knew too little.

Food offered the organizing principle of our time together, as was customary in our family. Over the course of several days I received a tutorial in the versatility of New Mexico's famous chile peppers. The state question, Dan told me, was three words long—*Red or green?*—and was usually asked in reference to that staple of New Mexican cuisine, enchiladas. Red sauce, smooth as velvet, was made of dried ripe chiles run through a blender and a sieve; green sauce took the form of a chunky broth built around fresh diced chiles. Either could run the gamut from mild to apocalyptic, and the hottest iterations, to which Dan was partial, had the potential to tear the roof off your mouth. We added raw chiles to our eggs at breakfast, and our aunt used them in an apple pie. My tolerance for spicy food, always high, helped me pass what I came to understand was a kind of test administered to the first-time visitor. We ate out most evenings, washed down our food with ice-cold Mexican beer and reposado tequila, and when the mood loosened Dan spoke of flying. That was to be the prize of the trip.

He told me about the annual balloon fiesta, the main event in the public life of Albuquerque and the largest gathering of its kind in the world, a tradition dating back more than twenty years. Each October several hundred balloonists ascended over the city while tens of thousands of spectators gathered to look skyward. Dan had been taken with the romance of flight from the moment he'd arrived in the city. He'd logged trainee hours for months to earn his pilot's license, flying almost every weekend with his boss. The Albuquerque weather was ideal for ballooning much of the year, with prevailing winds creating a phenomenon known as the box. Surface breezes typically blew one direction, upper elevation winds blew the other, a crosscurrent caused by temperature inversion and the geographic features of the valley, with mountains on the east, the big mesa on the west. A skilled balloonist could make use of the conflicting winds to take off and land in the same general area, avoiding an embarrassing trespass of private property or a nightmare descent in harsh terrain.

Dan liked to be in the air as early as possible, before the warmth of the sun stirred the wind, so we rose on a Saturday morning before dawn and dressed in haste. A pot of coffee, made on a timer, awaited pouring into a thermos. All other preparations had occurred the night before.

The air outside was brisk, scented with the unmistakable tang of the desert in winter. The horizon above the mountains had begun to glow like a coal. Four of us got in the truck and set off. We each took a turn at the thermos. I looked out the window at the pale, naked earth. My stomach felt sick from strong coffee and lack of sleep. I'd never been much of a morning person, another way in which Dan and I differed.

Dan turned the truck off pavement and followed a two-track road, a rooster tail of dust rising behind us. In the middle of a mesa he found an opening in which to park, and everyone set to work as if they'd done this a hundred times, which in fact they had, a mechanical ballet involving earth, wind, and sky, though I did not fully grasp it yet.

I helped my aunt Ruth lift the wicker basket out of the truck bed. My uncle Robert readied the gasoline-powered fan. Dan unrolled the envelope of the balloon on the face of the mesa, securing it to the basket with a series of cables. Once Robert had the fan running, Dan pointed it at the mouth of the balloon. The envelope began to fill with cold air, and he tugged on the cloth here and there to keep it from snagging as the panels of yellow, red, and blue fabric rippled like a flag in a big wind. I stood back, watching silently, feeling useless and a little bit awed. I wanted to offer help but I didn't know how, and Dan gave no sign that he needed any, so I stood with my hands in my pockets, trying to stay warm, trying to look ready but not too eager.

Dan lit the propane burner mounted above the basket. He fired off a horizontal sword of flame, slowly warming the air inside the balloon. The burner roared and went silent, roared and went silent. No one said a word. The balloon slowly stretched taut. Everyone looked up, at the balloon and the sky beyond it, the sword of flame now and then appearing in the balloon's mouth, until the silken bubble swung into place overhead.

Get in! my aunt Ruth yelled, as a gust of wind came up, the first of the morning. The urgency in her voice jarred me from my reverie. No time to grab the two-way radio for contact with the chase truck. No time to grab my camera to document the moment. No time to waste if I didn't want to miss the ride.

I got one leg over the edge as the basket made a lateral hop. It came to ground with a thud and hopped again, and I feared I'd lose my balance and tip over the side. Dan was working the burner, trying to achieve the requisite heat for lift-off, and I had one hand on the basket's edge and one hand raised behind my head like a bull rider for balance, waving a frantic goodbye to the ground, or what I hoped was goodbye and not hello, for in that moment it could have gone either way.

Dan grabbed the collar of my jacket and pulled hard, yanking me into the basket with him. For a second I crouched at his feet, breathing with quick little rasps of fear at how close I'd come to missing the ride. He looked down at me and laughed, shook his head. He hadn't expected the sudden wind and admitted as much. Still, he couldn't resist a poke at such an easy target.

Way to be quick on your feet, he said.

After a two-beat pause he added: You might want to stand up for this.

I rose and looked down at the world we were leaving

behind. Ruth waved up at us, a stick figure receding on the mesa; the mesa itself shrank to the size of a tabletop, then a postage stamp. The whole of Albuquerque slumbered in the cold light of sunrise, the dun-colored earth inscribed by the valley of the Rio Grande, a gray thread curling through the city's sere heart. The rugged spine of the Sandias loomed in the east, a sky island dark with pine in the upper elevations, stark contrast to the spare, lion-colored flora of the desert below. Across the valley to the west little conical peaks rose here and there like scale-model remnants of ancient volcanoes. From somewhere off in the distance I heard the faint bark of a dog. There were no other sounds but the burner and the breeze.

Two thousand feet below us suburban rooftops glinted like bits of confetti. Cars moved like tiny beetles, scuttling on the stems of the interstates. The entirety of the city had the look of a modular, mutant amoeba stretched across the surface of a pale brown sea. Ten minutes earlier I'd been an earthbound creature. Now I floated in the sky as if cupped in the talons of some magisterial bird. I was twenty-two years old and I'd never been in an airplane. I'd never defied gravity for longer than a bounce on a trampoline or a flop from a high-diving board. The grace of our lift into sky made me giddy. I pretended to shiver from cold even as I trembled with something like euphoria.

Dan's demeanor encouraged me to play it outwardly cool, though. He tended the propane burner with confidence, one hand slung free at his side, his face accented by his first real stab at a mustache, not shabby for a twenty-one-year-old.

He'd filled out in the time since I'd seen him last, gaining twenty pounds, much of it muscle. His calm self-assurance had nothing of a pose about it. He was clearly in his element. He pointed out the city's major landmarks: the university, the airport, the bosque along the river's course, the Old Town where we'd walked the day before through narrow streets hemmed by neat walls of adobe. I nodded and looked where he told me to, but from the corner of my eye I couldn't stop watching him. It was as if I were seeing him clearly for the first time in my life—no longer the eternal kid brother, but a man in his own right, possessed of a passion I'd barely known about until I was invited to share in its pleasures.

See the mountains over there? he asked, pointing at the Sandias. Someday I'm going to fly over them. Not many people have tried it. It takes a serious tailwind, and you have to be prepared for anything, because the wind shear on top can smash you to pieces on the other side. But I think it's worth the risk.

He continued looking that way for a moment, as if gaming it out in his head. I wanted to know more about the logistics of such a flight, but I couldn't think of what to ask, so I joined him in silent appraisal of the morning light on the mountains.

My joy lasted the entire ascent and more than half the descent. We drifted down and caught the low-level breeze again, moving lateral to the surface of the earth, then found a pocket of calm and drifted down some more. I looked away, looked at Dan. His concentration on the task at hand was total, both hands working the rope line running to the parachute vent in the top of the balloon, through which he let hot air escape.

I forgot to tell you, he said, looking upward through the mouth of the balloon. My friends nicknamed this thing the Cactus Plower. Landing is always the most interesting part.

He surveyed the ground below us, judging the suitability of potential landing zones. None of them looked soft. The earth was rising to meet us in a game of chicken we couldn't win. At some final point of surrender to wind and gravity he let go of the rope line to the parachute vent and braced his arms on the edge of the basket. I did likewise. I closed my eyes seconds before we came to ground, unable to bear the sickening wait for impact. The force of the landing made my teeth chatter. The basket tipped on its side; my body went momentarily airborne. When I opened my eyes I found myself curled in a ball, covered in the crusty soil of the desert. I brushed the dust from my jacket and squatted on my haunches, careful not to stand before my dizziness passed.

I muttered something about having had all the excitement I could handle in one day.

That's too bad, he said, because there's one more thing before you're legit.

Among hot air balloonists there was a baptismal tradition that Dan honored: when a person made his virgin flight, the rite of passage was marked with champagne, cases of which had been the ballast of choice for the earliest balloonists. Our aunt Ruth having tracked us down in the chase truck, the balloon having been packed and stowed, we drove back into the city. In Ruth and Robert's back yard I was told to kneel, hands behind my back, and bend toward a small paper cup placed on the ground in front of me. The idea was to grip the lip of the cup in my teeth and drink the champagne by lifting and tilting my head. Dan sat facing me, giving instructions. He insisted that I not use my hands, that I not leave my position until the cup was emptied in my mouth and set back on the ground with my teeth. I was a willing acolyte, eager to do anything he told me. I should have sensed the whole thing was a setup, meant to place me in a defenseless position. At the moment of my most intense concentration, when all I could see of the world was the cup attached to my face and Dan just beyond it, Ruth and Robert came forward and poured their glasses and the rest of the bottle over my head, and Dan doused me with his own glass for good measure. I roared up off my knees, shaking like a muskrat, dabbing with my shirtsleeve at the champagne in my eyes.

Welcome to the club, brother, he said.

We shared another cup from a spare bottle as I toweled off with my flannel shirt. Sticky with cheap bubbly, shivering in the late morning breeze, I felt my admiration for him blossom into something more powerful, almost disorienting, uncomfortably close to envy. Without any fuss or the least hint of self-congratulation, he'd shepherded me through an experience I already sensed would last in memory the rest of my life. The closer I looked at him, the more impressive he seemed. He had the kind of adult life I lacked, not to mention a major talent, bordering on artistry, that allowed him to rise above the world whenever he felt like it, assuming the wind was right. My undergraduate reality looked insubstantial by comparison, with its basement keg parties and communal living arrangements, the rah-rah silliness of Saturday afternoon football games. These feelings were so unexpected, so far from anything I'd ever felt about him, that I could not find the courage to express them, and anyway words of appreciation had never come naturally for either of us. We had been farm kids, after all, and emotional effusiveness was not our style, not by a long shot.

In my earliest memories there was no such thing as him or me, only us. Dan and I were born one year and nine days apart, and though I was the older I had no recollection of life before he appeared. Until I went to kindergarten at the age of five we were an inseparable pair, coconspirators unmindful of language, at home in the out of doors, amid the smells of sloughs and mud and skunks and manure. We snuck ripe strawberries from our mother's garden together, built snow forts in the windbreak of woods, swam and fished in the river, made up games of war, American boys on the American land. Growing up on a farm three miles from the nearest town, we each were all the other had, until our sister Lisa arrived three years after Dan and took her place as our mascot.

We knew early it was our destiny to be farmers. Our father farmed a rented homestead of a quarter section. His uncles farmed to the west and to the north. Our grandmother grew up on the farm where our great-grandfather spent his entire life, the original homestead claimed by our great-great-grandfather, in 1887. We were said to have descended from a Parisian pharmacist and grocer named Louis Hebert, who emigrated to Quebec early in the seventeenth century and became the man referred to in history books as "the first farmer of Canada." Dan and I would have been the fifth generation to work the soil in the same little corner of southwest Minnesota, Des Moines River headwaters country, on the western edge of what had once been the tallgrass prairie. The first object I can recall coveting was a shiny toy tractor with an enclosed cab, which I received for a birthday gift the year I turned four. We used it to practice growing corn in a patch of earth behind the garage. We tilled the soil and planted seeds snuck from bags in the granary; we weeded the rows and watered the plants until they'd grown to scale with our tractor. Then we cut and chopped our tiny stalks the way our father did for silage, and like our father we covered our piles with a swatch of black plastic to ferment them with the warmth of the sunlight, fodder for the cattle, to get them through the lean months till the grain came in from the fields.

It was an enchanting world in its way, as most childhood landscapes are: an agrarian paradise of rich post-glacial soil, with just a sliver of the old wildness remaining to invite you past the manicured fields of corn and beans, their rectilinear geometry. Marshlands and prairie pothole lakes dimpled the low spots in the land, and where the water still pooled and on its edges, along the drainage ditches that ran square as the rows of corn, in strips of untamed earth along the railroad right-of-way, some of the ancient prairie still survived. These remnants were sparse, though, and anyway our mission was to tame the land and bend it to our will and take our living from it. We didn't earn money by admiring it. That was a lesson imparted early.

Other lessons we learned by watching, still others we learned by doing. Our father needed the help. He was in deep with the bank from the beginning, having made his start with borrowed money, and he tended his own land while also helping his uncle on the home place down the road. As soon as we had muscles, he put them to work. We learned the toughest job first, picking rock, then later in the summer pulling weeds from the soybean fields. Rock-picking was springtime duty, before the crop was planted but after the fields were plowed. Someone drove a tractor with a loader bucket in front or a wagon hitched behind, or both, and we walked alongside it through the soft and yielding clods of overturned soil, hoisting anything bigger than a softball up into the pile. Rocks could damage the planter or, worse, the combine at harvest. Removing them was a preventative measure, a hedge against damaged machines and lost time, and among the most stupefying of labors ever performed by humans on earth. Giant cairns marked each corner of the rockiest fields, monuments to our labor and the labor of those before us. They had a simple beauty not at all in keeping with the brutality of the work that had formed them. The springtime winds chapped our lips, our hands cracked from digging in the dirt, but we knew better than to complain. Farming wasn't easy. We heard that often enough. Rocks and weeds and bad weather were the enemies, and since one of the three could not be controlled, we had to do our best where we were able. Farming tested a person; those found wanting failed. This was the ironclad law of the life we were born for.

My going to kindergarten a year before Dan nudged us apart, as did overheard jokes about our paternity, for though we were close in age we looked nothing alike, to the point where that was our most notable characteristic, the one people fixated on—our physical dissimilarity. Under "comments" in his baby book, our mother had written the first things said about him at birth, among them: *He's so different from Philip.* I had our mother's dark features, he had our father's strawberry blond hair and fair skin. Our personalities and interests formed as distinctly as our looks. I became a reader, asthmatic and sensitive, squeamish around farm animals, more comfortable baking cookies than baling hay. Early on he showed competence with his hands, unafraid to plunge his arm into a sow and extract a piglet, quicker to learn how to drive a tractor or run a grain auger, more instinctive with tools. Being the older brother meant never wanting to show weakness in his presence, so I scooped manure and castrated pigs alongside him, outwardly capable, inwardly doubtful. I'm sure anyone could have seen which of us was touched by a faint delicacy of manner, and anyway our 4-H projects told the tale. Dan always showed a hog at the county fair, while I played at artsier things—black-and-white photography, model airplanes.

The one thing we'd always taken for granted, that we would someday be farmers, became the one option unavailable to us the year I turned twelve. The bankers lost their patience; we held a sale, packed our things in boxes, and left the only home we'd ever known to the wind and time. We'd been found wanting, not in work ethic but in financial viability. Old Lady Leysen rented the land to a neighbor, and that was the end of another homestead. No one would ever live there again. The buildings would eventually be burned to the ground as part of a training exercise for the local volunteer fire department, leaving only a metal Quonset hut and a concrete silo as headstones to mark our failed efforts, the rest of the rooms of our childhood consumed in flame.

As much as I missed certain special places on the land, places where I felt the first tendrils of connection to things more enduring than the human-built world, I was also secretly relieved when we left. I'd never felt sure of myself in the more complicated work of the farm, never gained a feel for it, the way Dan had instinctively. A fresh chance at self-invention appealed to me. I can't say how Dan felt, though of course I can guess. I never asked, and he never said, but I had cause to wonder if in the loss of the farm he lost something of himself he could never recover.

As a teenager I became obsessed with sports. I trained for basketball and track in the humid clamor of the high school weight room; I pored over copies of the *Sporting News* after I finished my homework at night, dreaming of one day seeing my name in print, if only in the local sports pages. Dan focused his efforts on the wood shop, becoming skilled enough to hire on summers with his shop teacher, with whom he built furniture and cabinets. As a wrestler, he viewed my passion for basketball as something of a retreat from manlier pursuits. Insofar as my teenage mind believed anything with bedrock conviction, it was that the fast-break style of the Los Angeles Lakers in the Showtime years was the pinnacle of team-sport artistry, and Dan countered by claiming that the Detroit Pistons—known as the Bad Boys, for their intimidating physicality and brutish antics—were his favorite team. He spent the weekends tinkering with cars, an investment of time and energy that confounded me, since he would smash them up during races at the county fair each August, undoing all his hard work in a few loops around the track.

No one was surprised when I went away to college and he chose the path of blue-collar work. It was the natural move for each of us, and after he accepted our aunt and uncle's invitation to move to New Mexico and bunk with them while he got himself settled, he existed only on the far edge of my consciousness. We were brothers in our early twenties, each of us making his own way in the world, more than a thousand miles apart. I suspect he thought of me as infrequently as I thought of him.

After the champagne baptism, we drank beer and made dinner and spoke of work and school and other such pleas-antries. We played a game of Monopoly with Emily and her parents, settling into the banter of good-natured competition, affectionate teasing of the kind that made everyone around us laugh. The elation from our early morning flight continued to hum in my mind. The whole day had about it the character of a festive reunion. Beer flowed, old stories were retold, others told for the first time. Late in the evening, when Dan asked about my work as a reporting intern for the *Fargo Forum* the previous summer—our mother, he admitted, had sent him some of my clips—I had enough beer in me to tell him the truth, which was that the whole experience had been something of a farce.

One Monday morning, shortly after my feature on the city's pet groomers was splashed across the entire face of the B section, along with color photos of poodles and dachshunds undergoing various forms of makeover, I decided I'd had enough. One month remained of my internship, one month more than I could stand. I skipped breakfast and went straight to a sports-medicine clinic. To a kindly but perplexed nurse, I explained that I was with the drama department at the university. We were putting on a play in the fall, and in the play there was a character who wore a sling on his arm. Our prop room lacked a sling. I asked if she might let me borrow one, or, if that wasn't an option, whether she might take cash for it. She seemed to pity me for some reason, perhaps the transparency of my lie; she let me have the thing for free. I told her I'd stop by with a couple of complimentary tickets in the fall, before the play opened, and she pretended to sound pleased.

Half an hour later I appeared in the office of the managing editor, empty shirtsleeve dangling at my side like a flag of surrender. I explained my history of shoulder trouble (true), told him in detail how I'd dislocated it over the weekend in a game of pickup basketball (false), and informed him that I needed to leave immediately to see my doctor back in Minneapolis about the likelihood of major rotator-cuff surgery (preposterous). The old man stabbed out his cigarette and lit another, wheezing as he shifted his enormous girth in his chair. He peered at me over the top of his half-moon glasses.

I'm sorry, I said, but I can't stay. I can't even take notes anymore.

You can use a tape recorder, he said.

I don't have one.

We'll get you one.

But I can't even type, I said, wiggling my pathetic chicken wing for emphasis.

Sure you can, he said. You'll just have to use one hand. Hunt and peck. Half the monkeys in the newsroom type that way.

His arguments were futile. By noon I'd packed my car, having worn the sling the whole time in case a colleague from the paper drove past the empty frat house—Alpha Gamma Rho, the farm-boy fraternity—where I'd rented a room for the summer. I was thirty miles down Interstate 94, smoking a celebratory joint, when I remembered I wasn't really injured and didn't need the sling.

Hearing this, Dan snorted so hard that beer geysered out of his nose. He'd never thought of me as all that amusing, and though I'd done my best to leave out the boring parts of the story, I hadn't expected to hit his funny bone quite so squarely. His reaction proved contagious. We laughed until our faces were wet with tears. I couldn't remember the last time we'd done so. Maybe we never had.

The joint, he said. It was the joint. I can see you lighting it, no hands on the wheel.

Soon afterward, perhaps wanting to be funny in his turn, he mentioned—apropos of the coming holiday—that he planned to take an out-of-town trip over the long weekend, to a balloon rally in the northwest part of New Mexico, since he wouldn't have to work on Martin Luther Coon Day.

My shock was immediate and visceral. I wanted to believe I'd misheard him. Dan had a smirk on his face, a look of mischievous pride, that assured me I had not misheard. No one else seemed to notice or care. He may have thought it a harmless joke, but for me it was neither harmless nor a joke, so I went to the fridge and got another beer, then another as the conversation limped on. I performed some elaborate mental contortions to avoid placing the blame for the remark where it belonged, with the owner of the mouth that had uttered it. I settled on the notion that he was taking his cues on the postures of masculinity from the men he was hanging around at the time, men you might call, to be gracious about it, illiberal. With time and maturity he'd see the folly of their crude worldview. He'd shake off those bits of boilerplate prejudice he'd borrowed in the project of crafting a self and become his own man.

We returned to being out of the loop with each other the moment I left on the long drive home. When I arrived back at school that January I briefly considered sending him a note of thanks, along with a photocopy of "Letter from Birmingham Jail," but I figured he'd take it as a calculated insult, the high-minded snobbery of his college-boy brother, so I didn't bother with the essay or the note. Emily called off their wedding not long afterward, a fact relayed to me by my mother, so our plan to gather as a family that summer dissolved.

The following autumn my telephone rang at home. It was Dan, calling to catch up. We hadn't talked in most of a year. I was half drunk and in no mood for chitchat, so I lied and told him I was deeply invested in a *Monday Night Football* game. I told him I'd call him back at halftime and I hung up the phone. For reasons that remain obscure to me, although they surely had something to do with the words Martin Luther Coon Day, I never returned the call.

This would always remain the final exchange between us: his calling to connect, my turning away.

A few months later, on the day that turned out to be his last, I arrived in New York for a summer internship at the *Nation* magazine. I'd arranged the job in part so I could spend time with my girlfriend, who'd already graduated and left for New York ahead of me; it was also meant to be my springboard into an honest-to-god career, the last bit of polish on my résumé before I returned to Montana to finish my degree.

Marie and I had become involved after working on our college newspaper together. Amid late nights of intense work in a hothouse office, I'd fallen hard for her, in a way I hadn't for anyone in my life to that point. She was a smart editor, a varsity tennis player with the legs that entailed, fluent in French, with a daring sense of fashion shaped by a semester in Paris. With her hair cut short and a cigarette in her hand, she looked like the brunette twin of the movie starlet Jean Seberg, another midwestern girl with an air of irrepressible sensuality. She called me *chéri* and undertook to expose me to the spiritual dimensions of gourmet coffee and good red wine, an education I can only think to call erotic in its devotion to sensory pleasures, to smells and tastes and textures, most of them a major revelation for a descendant of the first farmer of Canada. Some nights, early in our courtship, we'd sneak away from the paper for a couple of hours, fix dinner at her place, share a bottle of Bordeaux, then return to the office to meet our deadline. Our attraction, shy and halting at first, was the headiest thing I'd ever been a part of, the affections we'd hidden from our colleagues, the long hours engrossed in the creation of something real—an actual newspaper—and of course the moment long after midnight when our work was done and we were finally alone. We had dreamed of New York even then, walking across campus together in the quiet of snowy nights, and now the summer was ours, the city was ours, a possibility I'd been imagining for a very long time.

After Marie and I had reacquainted, I called my mother to let her know I was in New York safely. We talked for a bit about my travels—I'd come by car all the way from Montana—and then she told me, with an edge of concern in her voice, that she'd talked to Dan earlier in the day, around lunchtime. He'd told her that his new girlfriend had decided to break things off. Wendy was ten years older than him and hadn't signed the papers on her divorce, and although her two kids liked Dan, they were confused by the sudden appearance of a man they couldn't help viewing as their father's replacement. Everything had happened too quickly between them, and she needed a break to put her life in order. My mother did her best to cheer him up, my father too, and when they hung up they figured he'd have a few bumpy weeks. Eventually he'd find someone else, someone more suitable, ideally unmarried and closer to his own age.

Still, my mother said, he sounded pretty down. It might cheer him up to hear from you.

I told her I'd call him.

I hung up the phone and thought, *Sure, I'll call him— silly kid brother and his silly troubles with women. I'll call him in a few days. Next week, maybe.* I'd been reunited with Marie for a couple of hours. We'd spent nine months apart, writing letters across the distance between us, and to find myself at last within reach of her touch made me want nothing else. Anything aside from that could wait.

The next morning I went to the offices of the magazine, thinking it was going to be my first day on the job, not having received the news that the interns' start date had been moved back one day, unaware it would be more than a year before I'd return for my internship, by which time Marie would be gone for Paris again, our love but a memory. I spent an hour at the office, met some of the editors, grabbed a stack of back issues. In possession of a free afternoon I hadn't expected to be free, I was at a loss for what to do with myself. The city seemed huge and half mad, a roiling carnival of commerce, an immense performance of human longing. I called Marie from a pay phone. We made a dinner plan, a celebration of our reunion. I walked all over Lower Manhattan, tuning in to the pace of street life, browsing amid the evocative, moldering-book smell of the Strand. I found an open bench in Union Square and unfolded a copy of the *Times*—my new hometown paper. Tears of happiness welled in my eyes as I sat there on that bench. Everything had come together, exactly as we'd planned it.

Late that afternoon, in the final minutes of my innocence, when he was already gone and I didn't know it, I puttered around Marie's apartment in Queens, listening to her Rickie Lee Jones albums, holding her clothes to my face, savoring the scent of her, delirious with longing. I was getting dressed for my first-ever dinner in Manhattan when the telephone rang.

I muted the Rickie Lee Jones. I picked up the phone. I knew from my father's quavering voice that whatever he was about to tell me would change everything.

The known facts were these:

He'd spent the afternoon with friends, drinking.

He'd spoken to Wendy in the evening by phone.

He hadn't shown up for work the next morning.

He'd died alone in his apartment.

He'd done the deed with a gun.

. . . .

The week surrounding the burial was a maelstrom of tears and bewilderment and wild speculation about what had gone so wrong inside his head that he would choose to point a gun at it, and most of that time, mercifully, remains a fog in my memory. One moment stood out, though, a moment that would define my life in the years to come. It happened on the afternoon of the wake, when one of my uncles, in a moment of thoughtless candor, told me that if the family had been forced to choose ahead of time which of us was more likely to off himself, the odds would've favored me. At first I had no idea what to make of this extraordinary statement, except to wonder whether everyone's sorrow might have been a little less intense, a little less violent, if the death had been mine. People said a lot of foolish things in the midst of their initial shock, but this one stayed with me: the idea that I'd bucked the odds and lived. In moments of self-pity, I allowed myself to wonder whether I'd failed the family by not performing to expectations. Viewed from a different angle, my uncle's words offered up the rest of my life as an unexpected gift, an opportunity for the most radical improvisation. I could be whatever I wanted to be, as long as I didn't end up another corpse in the casket with a hole in his head. Anything went. Anything was permissible, as long as I lived.

It soon became clear that the manner of his death had turned him into something of a cipher. People saw him one way or the other: sufferer or coward, victim or murderer. He either succumbed to outside forces or succumbed to the darkest impulse within. In the days after his death, when people's explanations were forming and quickly hardening—little stories they thought they could live with—I often felt I was the only one who vacillated between the two extremes, pitying him one hour and hating him the next. Everyone else, it seemed, had chosen, or was clinging to a brave front of certainty. The gunshot was a mistaken impulse, the gunshot was a calculated rebuke. He slipped over the edge, he was pushed over the edge. He was broken by a battle with depression, he was broken by the sudden loss of love. He clung too tightly to other people, he didn't know how to reach for help. The list of explanations was as long as the list of people who'd known him, and each seemed to me a simplification, perhaps even a lie.

I understood these accounts were attempts by those who loved him to soothe the pain of a sudden, inexplicable absence, but I took it as my duty to preserve some ambiguity, if for no other reason than to allow him an inner life of some complexity, resistant to easy answers and summary judgments. I hoped that time and patience would one day reward me with the truth but I was in no hurry to get there. The question for me was never, *Why did he kill himself?* He killed himself, I assumed, because his life became unbearable. The question, therefore, was why his life had become unbearable, and since I knew very little about his life at the end, and even less about his frame of mind, I couldn't answer that question, and maybe never would. The proximate cause of his suicide—the breakup of an eight-month relationship—struck me as both too pat and maddeningly sketchy, a combination that led me to fixate on his final moments, improvising on the known facts, searching for a way into the mystery. I imagined his final hours again and again, long after a finer mind would have found peace or given up. I didn't want to find peace. To have found peace, I thought, would have meant giving up my obsession with him, but that obsession had become the one thing that gave my life meaning.

The evening meals I shared with my parents that summer in Minnesota were funereal, as was only appropriate. To speak was to invite the possibility of invoking his name, and his name was just then unutterable, though he was always in our thoughts. In the beginning those thoughts focused on the last time we saw him, the last time we spoke to him; we hunted for clues we should have seen and didn't, or we tried ourselves on the charge of failing to love him sufficiently, a trial that couldn't help but end in a verdict of guilt. My sister, with whom I'd always been able to speak freely on any subject, was deep inside the drama that would result in a brief, failed marriage, and therefore unavailable for sibling heart-to-hearts. I knew better than to hope that my mother and father would look deep into each other's souls, reaffirm their vows of fidelity in the face of tragedy, and draw me into the safe, warm bosom of their loving embrace. Never having been the kind of people who spoke freely—or even elliptically—about their innermost feelings, they weren't about to start now, when the stakes were so much higher. My father soon devised a mantra—life was too short to dwell on a death he could not undo—that baffled me with what I took to be its refusal to feel a legitimate sadness; my mother's devastation revealed itself wordlessly, with an expression of almost complete vacancy in her eyes, as if she'd gone somewhere in her mind from which she would never return. Their estrangement from each other's experience of grief was too painful for me to contemplate it for more than a moment, so I turned away from them, turned inward—a strategy that became a habit, a habit that became a posture, a posture that solidified into an all-encompassing personality, that of a man shrouded in almost total self-regard.

The ambiguity I preserved in the story of his death was already on its way to becoming the story of my life. He was my silent partner, my all-purpose excuse, my left-hand man, and depending on my whim I was sometimes calculating, sometimes impulsive, one minute attentive and the next minute aloof, one day hungry for intimacy and the next day desperate for freedom. By remaining enigmatic—by refusing to be any one way or any one thing—I honored him. He would remain forever unfinished, and so would I.

PART TWO

Fax Boy

My address was the movie house, downtown Missoula, on the banks of the Clark Fork. The yellow marquee glowed outside my bedroom window, and night after night an early and a late show played through the wall of the balcony across the hall. I read novels till dawn, slept till noon, napped around seven each evening with plugs in my ears to keep the movies muted. I walked the river paths after dark. I lurked in AA meetings in order to hear people talk honestly about terrible things. I drank coffee in one of three coffee shops each afternoon, whiskey in one of five bars most nights. I went months without having a conversation lasting more than three minutes. I swam through time like it was motor oil. I made one promise to myself. I would not buy a gun.

I took a semester off and returned to New York on borrowed money, my first cash advance on my first credit card. I sublet an apartment in Queens whose occupant, an Italian man in his thirties, was laid up in the hospital with two broken legs. I didn't ask why.

I completed my aborted internship at the *Nation*—a year and a half later than originally planned—for the sum of one hundred bucks a week, a willingly indentured servant at a magazine founded by abolitionists. I spent my days fact-checking articles on how to reinvigorate the labor movement, a staple of *Nation* reportage whose frequency and desperation of tone increased as union membership declined. During lulls between deadlines I gathered specious research for a contrarian columnist on what he called the hoax of global warming.

Back in Missoula, I worked on my pool game at Flipper's, my drinking game at Al's & Vic's. One day I received a piece of paper in the mail saying that I'd earned a bachelor's degree. I couldn't have begun to tell you how.

Lacking immediate prospects after graduation, I stayed on in Montana. There was no urgency to make anything of my life, and Missoula was as fine a place as any to hide out from postgrad choices. Besides, the place was too beautiful to leave in summertime, and I couldn't bear to give up an apartment that cost $180 a month and placed me within easy walking distance of so many quality bars. On summer days fishermen cast their flies upstream from the Higgins Avenue Bridge, a hundred yards from my room above the Wilma, while a bagpiper went through his mournful musical paces, using the bridge abutments as acoustic enhancement. I eked out a living baking bread in the early morning hours alongside a failed novelist who'd mastered the texture of the baguette, though not the art of fiction, during two years in Paris in the 1970s. Afternoons in my apartment, with the windows thrown open to the breeze off the black cottonwoods along the river, I worked halfheartedly on what I hoped would become my own first novel, a doomed imitation of Paul Auster's *New York Trilogy* that stalled forever at page forty with the impossible scenario of a man tailing the ghost of himself after digging up his own grave and finding nothing in it. I felt authentically bohemian as I pounded on my manual typewriter, earplugs in place, while the muffled soundtrack of the week's feature film pulsed and droned through the wall. One of the theater employees was a daytime drinker who liked to stop by my room in the late afternoons and slyly proposition me, vodka fumes on his breath. He probably did so with all the bachelor boys, but I was vain enough, and lonely enough, to take it as a compliment. The building's manual elevator, one of the few of its kind still in operation west of the Mississippi, was staffed in part by a woman who'd never abandoned the apartment upstairs where her husband had shot himself a decade earlier, or so the rumor went. Riding the lift with her after a night out drinking, I fantasized about holding her hand in mine and telling her she was not alone. More than once I heard another rumor that David Lynch had spent some time around the place, long enough to use it as a model for the apartment building in *Blue Velvet*. Once you'd lived there awhile, the story had the ring of plausibility, though of course it turned out to be a fabrication.

Every so often, when I felt myself slipping into a neurasthenic funk, I'd walk to the Orange Street entrance ramp on I-90 and hitchhike to Seattle to visit my uncle, hoping a brush with danger would snap me back to reality. Nothing very interesting happened on those trips, except for the time I was aggressively solicited to proffer my cock so my driver could fondle it with his right hand while steering with his left. He claimed all he wanted was to touch my cock for awhile, then pull off the road and finish the job with his mouth. For this he'd drive me all the way to Seattle from the Idaho border. When I demurred, he stuck his thumb in his mouth and removed his dentures, allowing them to dangle in the space between us. He said, with real conviction, *It'll be the best damn blow job you ever had.*

For a time I convinced myself that I'd given up on journalism. Life was too weird for journalism. I wanted to devote myself to art, to a bleak and eccentric vision along the lines of David Lynch. But the fact was I'd borrowed twenty-five grand to pay for an education in print journalism, so I had little choice but to pursue a career in print journalism, in order to pay off the twenty-five grand. Baking bread for six bucks an hour in Missoula, Montana, was not going to cut it, and there was nothing else I was any good at.

New York beckoned once more.

My first apartment in the city was a Hell's Kitchen sublet arranged on my behalf by a friend. An actress owned the apartment; she'd gone to some backwater city in the American South to appear in a Shakespeare festival. I covered her co-op payments and looked after her cats while she was away. There were four of them. Three had come off the streets, and their ways had rubbed off on the fourth, so that all were now at least part feral. Perhaps they felt abandoned by their owner, perhaps they just didn't like me, but they ceased to use their litter box, or rather they made the entire apartment their litter box. I chased them around with a broom, tried to frighten them into behaving, but that only provoked them to new outrages. I came home one night and found they'd torn apart my pillow, now just a cloudscape of synthetic stuffing floating across the bedroom floor. From then on I made my home away from home at McHale's, a bar off the west edge of Times Square, four blocks from my apartment.

The hamburger at McHale's was the best in the city, the bartenders—all of them female and all of them comely—poured spirits with a heavy hand, and the stools felt as if they'd been designed by ergonomic specialists devoted to the comfort of the human rump. Soft orange lamps burned dimly through the cigarette haze, and ceiling fans spun languidly in the sepia-toned light. I went there more than once in the daytime, but it was a bar built for the needs of the night. It was a hangout for off-duty cops and neighborhood residents and people who worked in the theater district, grips and lighting people and understudies and even the occasional name actor. It had the feel of a place that had been in the family for a very long time, as I later learned it had: half a century, to be precise. Ticket scalpers used it as a drop-off point, so there was a lot of traffic in and out, people leaning over the bar and offering their names, leaving with envelopes slipped in purses and pockets, a trade that gave the place a casually illicit flavor. I liked it in part because the help had a masterful sense for the balance of friendliness and discretion. The one thing they felt a need to know about you was your name. All the rest unfolded in conversation if you felt like talking. If you didn't, that was fine too. No one there knew my story, which was just as well. Nobody could vouch for me, or badmouth me, as long as I avoided romantic entanglements with the regulars. For a while, avoiding romantic entanglements became my highest priority, next to finding a job.

I sent my résumé to two dozen magazines and a handful of newspapers. I was summoned for an interview just once, a courtesy I was granted because I knew someone who knew someone who worked at the magazine. It was called *Civilization* and was affiliated with the Library of Congress. A secretary guided me to the office of the editor, Nelson Aldrich, who asked me about my internships. I told him of the meticulous fact-checking I'd done at the *Nation*, the intrepid street-level reporting I'd done during my summer at the *Fargo Forum*, the many things I'd learned about the ways of the world while staring into the abyss of an impending deadline. I must have gone too far with the self-marketing, because Nelson Aldrich said I was overqualified. He was looking for an editorial assistant—a gofer, essentially. I told him I really wanted the job, wanted the chance to be part of an organ of substantive journalism, even if only as a gofer. He said I'd probably find the work boring and he didn't want a bored assistant moping around the office. I told him it wasn't my style to mope in the workplace. He told me the pay was poor and I could almost certainly find something better. I told him I'd already been looking for two months and didn't share his optimism. We spent most of the interview in this way—me begging in an unseemly manner for the job, him trying to talk me out of wanting it.

After I left his office I never saw him again.

I may have had to leave the city a failure if I hadn't called the head of the journalism department at the University of Montana. Before retreating to academia, Frank Allen had worked at the *Wall Street Journal*, so I figured he knew some people in New York who could lend me a hand. He'd been kind to me as a transfer student, helping me match classes I'd already taken with a new curriculum, and now he gave me the name of an editor at the *Journal*, told me I should call her and ask her to coffee. The thinking was that she might know someone who was willing to take a chance on a hungry young journalist from the northern plains.

Francine Schwadel oversaw the paper's legal-affairs coverage. We met on the mezzanine level of the paper's home building at 200 Liberty Street, just across West Street from the World Trade Center towers. Sitting at a tiny table with a faux-marble surface, a paper cup of coffee in her hand, Francine Schwadel said, in her gravelly Brooklyn accent, that Frank Allen had hired her when he was chief of the Philadelphia Bureau of the *Wall Street Journal*, and for that she was eternally grateful. There was no longer a Philadelphia Bureau of the *Wall Street Journal*, and about that she was sad.

She asked me a few questions about my experience, my goals, and then she said, Well, young man, my time is short, but your timing is awfully good. I've just been given clearance to hire a news assistant. Would you be interested in the job?

Yes, I said. Of course.

She told me to send her a résumé, cover letter, and six samples of my writing by the end of the week.

When I left the interview, which I hadn't even known was going to be an interview—I thought she'd give me the names of some people she knew, and I'd have coffee with them too, and they'd give me the names of other people with whom I'd have coffee, and I'd follow the chain of connections until someone offered me a job—I was conflicted. All of a sudden I had a chance for a job at a paper that considered itself the world's most important publication, but I didn't want to work at the world's most important publication. Journalism had appealed to me, in the beginning, because I'd been told by one of my professors that it was among the surest means of comforting the afflicted and afflicting the comfortable. To an idealistic undergrad with socialist inclinations, that chestnut made journalism sound both noble and fun, but of all the places for a young man on the make to pursue a career in journalism, the *Wall Street*

Journal seemed about the least compatible with a desire to comfort the afflicted and afflict the comfortable.

I had a problem, though, and it wasn't politics, which had begun to matter a lot less than the growing balance on my credit card. The legal-affairs editor wanted to see six samples of my writing, but I had only four, maybe five good ones from my days as an intern at North Dakota's largest daily newspaper. I didn't want to fall back on clips from my student newspaper days. The piece of which I was fondest was an essay I had written for the *Nation* about a proposed open-pit gold mine on the Blackfoot River in western Montana. In a throwaway line about a logging company whose clear-cuts of healthy forest had fouled the river with silt and killed untold numbers of fish, I'd written the following: "Even a newspaper as sympathetic to corporate plunder as the *Wall Street Journal* once called Plum Creek the 'Darth Vader of the timber industry.'" I doubted the legal-affairs editor thought of her employer as sympathetic to corporate plunder. And I very much doubted she would hire me if she discovered I'd written such a thing.

I suppose I could have laughed it off as a youthful indiscretion with the English language if she asked but I didn't want to take that chance. I had an acquaintance I trusted at the *Nation* and I called him, explained my situation, and asked if he'd do me a giant favor. Would he open the electronic archive of the magazine, touch up my article that said unkind things about the *Wall Street Journal,* and then print for me a copy of the doctored article, which would no longer say unkind things? At first he was reluctant. He didn't want to tinker with the historic record of the magazine. I told him he should of course change back my wording before saving and closing the file.

Not exactly the sort of thing I'd been taught in J-school, but he complied.

Shortly afterward, I was hired.

I showed up for my first day of work wearing a starched white shirt and a sober red tie, wanting to make a good impression. The first order of business was to get my picture taken and affixed to a magnetic pass card. When waved in front of a beam of discerning red light, the pass card unlocked security doors in the paper's austere corridors. Later I would learn that before the paper moved to the World Financial Center it did not have locked doors in its hallways, and one day a senior executive had returned from his lunch to find a sample of human feces on his desk chair. When the paper moved to its new headquarters, the executive insisted on the installation of locked doors that could only be unlocked with special pass cards. In theory a security measure, the pass cards also allowed the paper to track the movements of individual employees as they circulated through the hallways, thereby discouraging anyone who might have had a hankering to leave a malodorous turd on an executive's desk chair.

As a news assistant, I mainly fetched faxes and replenished empty water coolers. I spent most of each day standing over a squadron of fax machines, collating and stapling press releases and court documents, then delivering them to reporters who covered corporate law, telecommunications, and the various health care industries. I performed this task with actuarial efficiency, the paper a blur in my hand like a magician's trick; I served the reporters their faxes with the cordial discretion of a headwaiter in an uptown restaurant. The best means I had of telling good days from bad was by noting, at the end of my shift, whether or not I'd avoided a paper cut.

I'd spent my late teens and early twenties working dismal jobs—donut fryer, bartender, UPS package unloader—and borrowing heavily to pay for a college education that qualified me for a job that was already obsolete. People didn't need to send faxes anymore. They could send email. I thought about mentioning this to Francine Schwadel. Could we not encourage people to send their documents electronically, thereby saving the world lots of paper and me lots of time? But then I wondered whether that would result, a little too efficiently, in my own obsolescence. So I kept my mouth shut, sorted and stapled the faxes, and every two weeks cashed my paycheck, which still came quaintly on paper, despite the advent of direct deposit.

One day my phone rang at work. It was my friend Mary, who'd put me in touch with the actress sublessor, she of the feline-occupied apartment. Mary was feeling a little chagrined about the cats and wanted to make things right. She said she had a lead on another apartment. A friend of hers was moving to New York from Detroit. The friend from Detroit had recently visited the city and, while staying with people she knew in Brooklyn, was shown a lovely old brownstone apartment. The landlord, being bisexual and living on the premises, sought tenants who were gay, bisexual, or gay-friendly. The woman from Detroit happened to be a lesbian; being a homo-friendly straight guy, I was deemed a suitable candidate to be her roommate, at least by Mary's reckoning.

Mary was a writer, young and fledgling but with obvious talent. We'd met at the *Nation* and talked in an easy way from the moment I showed interest in her work. She had introduced me to the poetry of Theodore Roethke, a good thing to have in a dark time. I sensed early on that Mary wanted to be more than friends. She only made this clearer as time passed, and with each manic flutter of her eyelids I wondered: What could be so wrong with her that she found *me* attractive? I didn't want to be Mary's boyfriend. I wanted to be Mary's friend. She'd been kind to me when no one else had; she was among the few people who'd taken an interest in me in that lonely city.

On my computer at work I could enter any street address in America and retrieve census tract data in a couple of clicks—one of the many slick tools available to editorial employees of the *Journal*. I typed the number and the street name I'd been given, and onto my screen came a statistical snapshot of the neighborhood. A median family income barely half the national average. More than a third of residents with incomes below the poverty line. A population quantified like this:

American Indian—0
Asian—0
Black—4,294
Hispanic—162
White—13

At first I thought there'd been a misprint. Thirteen of my hue in a sample of almost 4,500? A minority population of 99.71 percent? The numbers didn't seem plausible. Then again, almost everywhere I'd ever lived—Iowa, Minnesota, Montana—the ratio of white to black had been reversed. If I was as broad-minded as I thought I was, what did I care if I was in the minority for once?

As I considered the merits of a move to Bedford-Stuyvesant, I sensed an opportunity to achieve, among other things, a kind of experiential compensation for my job. Every day my employer published a record of the news that was about the length of a short novel, and the version of reality contained in those pages, while interesting and even sometimes useful to the degree you had money lying around—and often most enlightening for the unspoken assumptions undergirding its conventional wisdom—bore almost no resemblance to the world I confronted day-to-day, and left out most of what interested me. It aimed to be the indispensable read for the rich and the reactionary, of which I was neither. The saying about the place was that you got two papers for the price of one: a respectable, often hard-hitting news section that glorified and scrutinized titans of commerce and empire, and a piss-and-vinegar editorial page that acted as the bullhorn for the interests of the moneyed class and the Republican Party. Some reporters I knew refused to read the editorials on principle, as if to acknowledge their existence was to admit that they tainted the integrity of the paper's reporting. Merely to mention the editorial page in the newsroom was to elicit a chuckle or a grimace, as if you'd audibly passed gas. My own embarrassment was intensified by the fact of my peonage. My duties were unrelated to any notion of integrity. I was a fax ferrier, a nobody, the guy whose most important task was to ensure that the water cooler didn't run dry in the middle of the day. To say I worked in news was only accurate to the extent that I worked in a newsroom; I had nothing to do with the pursuit of news.

One morning I showed up at work to find a message on my telephone from a man named Peter Brinch. He said he was a friend of Frank Allen's and was calling because he had a tip he wanted to share with a journalist. Frank Allen had kindly told him to call me.

I immediately called him back. I didn't tell Brinch that I wasn't a practicing journalist. Nor did I tell him that what the public thinks of as a good tip is often not news at all. There was a hint of sophistication in his voice that made me think he might tell me something extraordinary, something that would change the flat-line trajectory of my so-called career.

Brinch told me that he knew a man with an obsession for McDonald's.

That didn't sound promising. People obsessed about all sorts of things, and their obsessions were not news. They were just obsessions, some of them mildly intriguing, most of them pointless or creepy or sad.

Brinch continued: This guy has made it his life's goal to eat at as many McDonald's restaurants as possible. So far he's eaten at more than ten thousand of them, most in the United States, a few in Canada and the Caribbean. He's been to many that no longer exist. He started eating at McDonald's in the 1970s. Name any town or city in the U.S., and this guy can tell you whether it has a McDonald's, and if so how many, and where they're located. He has a photographic memory. He takes all his vacations in places where he hasn't eaten at the McDonald's yet. He considers his visits to new McDonald's a form of collecting. Collecting the McDonald's experience, he calls it. He makes notes on every restaurant he visits. He's never told his story to any-one. But I think he might be ready to talk.

Brinch told me the guy's name, which was Peter as well—Peter Holden—and he passed along Holden's phone number.

I thanked him for the tip.

I think it would make a good A-hed story, I really do, Brinch said before hanging up.

An A-hed was a story that ran in column four on the

front page of the *Wall Street Journal* every weekday—
a light-hearted, often humorous story that readers loved
because it represented an island of levity within a sea of
more serious news. Editors called it the A-hed because the
box around the two-deck headline above it was shaped like
a square-topped A.

It occurred to me, after I hung up with Brinch, that the
A-hed was often about someone's weird obsession.

During my lunch break I called Peter Holden. He told me
he worked for a data-imaging company in Virginia. He
explained that his firm scanned documents and compiled
them in databases that people could peruse with computers.
This eliminated the need to replicate documents in paper
form, and therefore saved a lot of trees.

Holden told me he was coming to New York on business the following week. We agreed to meet for lunch at a
McDonald's near the newspaper's office in Lower Manhattan. He said he had red hair and a brown briefcase. He
offered no other particulars about his appearance, but I
made the natural assumption. When I arrived at the restaurant, I looked for the fattest man in the place, but the fattest
man in the place did not have red hair or a brown briefcase.
The only man with red hair and a brown briefcase was tall,
trim, and looked about forty-five years old. Holden had told
me he was fifty-three.

We shook hands, ordered lunch. He was friendly, a little
bit shy of his achievement, and a little bit proud beneath

the shyness, prouder as the lunch wore on. He ate two Quarter Pounders with cheese—no onions—and drank a large Coke. I ate a Big Mac Value Meal with fries, drank a Hi-C Orange. He said that when I'd first called, he couldn't believe a reporter would have interest in a story such as his. Then he realized that if *The Guinness Book of World Records* had an entry for solo visits to McDonald's, he would almost certainly own it. As a token of thanks for my interest, he wanted to pay for both of our meals. I told him he couldn't do that; I would have to pay for both meals. At first he resisted, but I told him it was journalistic protocol. A reporter could never accept gifts from potential sources or subjects, even if the gift was only a Big Mac Value Meal: Journalism Ethics 101, avoiding the appearance of a quid pro quo.

Holden showed me several folders full of notes about his visits to McDonald's. I looked at the number for the most recent entry: 10,892.

That's not even all of the ones I've visited, he said. For years I went to McDonald's without taking notes. Only after I'd been to a thousand or so did I start.

I asked him to tell me how many McDonald's there were in Fargo, North Dakota, and he did. I asked him how many McDonald's there were in Missoula, Montana, and he listed them by the names of the streets they were on.

I asked him why he started doing this—collecting the McDonald's experience. He said that by the 1970s he'd visited every state capital and national park in the U.S. of A. He'd collected them all, from Montpelier and Cheyenne to

Montgomery and Santa Fe, Glacier, Zion, Gettysburg, the Everglades. I wondered what else there was to do, he said. So I thought I'd try to eat at every McDonald's. But they built them faster than I could get to them all.

He said his one-day record for visits to McDonald's was forty-five. He'd accomplished this in the suburbs of Detroit. Partway through that epic day he bought cookies for the road, since a visit didn't count unless he ate something from the restaurant, although the actual eating didn't have to happen in the restaurant.

At the conclusion of our lunch, I invited him up for a tour of the newspaper. He seemed delighted by the fact that I could wave a little pass card with my picture on it, and doors in the hallways of the *Wall Street Journal* would open for me. He asked me what subjects I covered for the paper. I was ashamed to admit I sorted faxes and replenished water coolers, so I told him I was a special research assistant to reporters who wrote about law, telecommunications, and the various health care industries. As we circulated through the maze of cubicles in the newsroom, I made sure to avoid the wing of the tenth floor where people knew me.

I told him his story was fascinating, a kind of quest story of a uniquely American kind. If my editor gave the go-ahead, perhaps I'd visit him where he lived, in Virginia, and we'd try to find a McDonald's somewhere in the vicinity, ideally a McDonald's he hadn't visited yet, although that seemed unlikely.

. . . .

I first saw Bed-Stuy after dark, so I hardly saw it at all. The C train carried me from the glassy chill of the Financial District to the Kingston–Throop stop on Fulton Street, and from there I walked the dozen blocks to Monroe Street, just off Marcus Garvey Boulevard. It was raining when I got off the train. Everyone hurried along the sidewalks hunched with umbrellas and newspapers over their heads, their knees bent in semi-crouch. With our hands up and our heads down, we looked like we were fleeing the wrath of something horrible come down from heaven.

The walk was long, fifteen minutes from the subway. The neighborhood was mostly residential, street after street of beautiful old brownstones, bodegas here and there on the avenues, an occasional barbershop or storefront church. The landlord answered the door when I rang. He introduced himself as Ben. He was a sharp-looking man, bald-headed, thirtyish, from Trinidad, with a suave but laid-back British Island accent. He lived on the top floor of his three-story brownstone. A lesbian couple lived on the ground floor, and the middle floor was open. The place was lovely: high ceilings, decorative molding, a claw-footed tub, two bedrooms and a decent-sized kitchen. I looked the place over. Ben looked me over. I'd come straight from work wearing a blue dress shirt, a red tie, and a black corduroy overcoat. I tried hard to appear a gay-friendly dude who'd pay his rent on time.

Mary tells me you work at the *Wall Street Journal*, he said.

It's true. I'm pretty sure I'm the only socialist there.

So you don't mind situations in which you're the outsider, he said.

I think that's safe to say, I said.

He gave me an application to fill out, told me he'd check my references and get back to me afterward.

You come as a friend of a friend of a friend, he said. It's probably yours if you want it, but let me do my due diligence.

When I told Francine Schwadel about Peter Holden, she thought I was kidding. She asked if I could verify his claim to have visited 10,892 McDonald's. I said, No, not exactly, but he showed me some of the notes he took about them and he seems pretty trustworthy.

That's not good enough, she said. We need absolute proof. If you can prove it, I think we've got a story.

I called Holden. I told him I needed to see copies of his notes from all 10,892 of his visits to McDonald's.

He said that would be impossible. Each collection of notes ranged from a few sentences to half a page or more. It would take him forever to make copies.

I asked if he could use his company's technology, scan the notes, and create for me a searchable database.

He said he didn't think he could use the company's technology for personal business.

I reminded him I was a reporter at the *Wall Street Journal*. We needed solid sources. We verified facts before putting them in the paper.

He said, Why don't I send the last three thousand entries

or so, and you can look through them and send them back? They're all numbered. I didn't start at five thousand. Come to think of it, I'll send you some from the beginning and some from the middle and some from the end.

I ran this by Francine Schwadel.

Tell him we'll pay to have them shipped, she said.

When they arrived, I took them home and spent an evening with them. Their banal repetition had a strange poetry to it, a kind of Whitmanesque list-making for the end of the millennium; in almost every instance he'd noted what he'd eaten, and the thought of all those empty calories, millions and millions of them, staggered me. All that ground-up cow flesh. All that corn syrup. All that time spent breathing the oleaginous air of the nation's McDonald's franchises.

The next morning I showed the notes to Francine Schwadel. I told her about my idea to visit Holden where he lived and take him to a McDonald's he'd not yet seen. I'd discovered the existence of a new one not far from his home, just across the state line in Maryland.

That way, I said, I'll be there for breaking news.

Very clever, she said, grimacing. Write me a proposal and I'll send it on to the page-one desk. I'll see if they'll let you travel. Don't get your hopes up. And tell your guy not to talk to any other reporter, anywhere, until your story runs.

After approval came down from page one, I was instructed to book a Friday evening train to Washington with my own credit card. I was needed at the fax machines during regular work hours, and as a greenhorn I would not be allowed to report on company time, though all my expenses would be reimbursed. For someone of my position, reporting was an extracurricular activity.

I'd learned some tricks about the various strategies one could employ from listening to the reporters around me. The guy in the cubicle to my left had the manner of a no-nonsense dentist. He was blunt and demanding, all business, insisting that he didn't want to waste anyone's time, so why beat around the bush, just tell me what I want to know and I won't bother you again—and people did. The woman in the cubicle across from me adopted the pose of a hopeless neophyte, confused, in over her head. She asked for things she pretended not to understand to be repeated, slower this time, like you're talking to your adolescent niece—and people did. Sometimes she laughed to herself after hanging up, amused by her own performance. She ought to have been. She broke news on all sorts of sophisticated Wall Street shenanigans and she got a lot of her leads by sounding like a complete ditz on the telephone.

With Holden I simply shut up and listened, nodded and ah-hummed a lot, and took page after page of notes as he extemporized. On a muggy Saturday morning we drove to a new McDonald's in College Park, Maryland. From the moment we stepped inside he smiled with childlike enthusiasm, his head swiveling as he tried to take it all in. The seating area had plastic tabletops laminated with the University of Maryland shield, and the walls were emblazoned with the words MARYLAND TERRAPINS.

Look at this, Holden exclaimed. I love this stuff!

He told me his greatest excitement in life came from finding a McDonald's restaurant with something slightly different about it, since most were carbon copies. He thanked me profusely for leading him to a version that was one of a kind, and for sharing in the joy of the discovery. We stayed no more than half an hour; the place was jammed with customers, and it didn't feel right to linger merely to admire the tabletops, the walls.

That afternoon he showed me around his home in suburban Virginia. Each room contained a different collection of some object: African masks in the living room, Russian nesting dolls in the dining room, and so on, dozens and dozens of each particular thing. In its museumlike tidiness, it looked like the kind of place a fastidious serial killer might call home. I couldn't stop myself from picturing a collection of severed body parts somewhere in the attic—thumbs, ears.

Are you a collector of anything? he asked.

About to say no, I thought of the commonplace book I'd been keeping. If I'd wanted to disturb him even more than he'd disturbed me, I could have quoted some of the entries. Pavese: *No one ever lacks a good reason for suicide.* Jong: *It was easy enough to kill yourself in a fit of despair. . . . It was harder to do nothing.* Freud: *No neurotic harbors thoughts of suicide which are not murderous impulses against others redirected upon himself.* Nietzsche: *The thought of suicide is a great consolation: with the help of it, one has got through many a bad night.* Pliny the Elder: *Amid the miseries of our life on earth, suicide is God's gift to man.* Artaud:

If I commit suicide, it will not be to destroy myself but to put myself back together again. And so on. I assumed that counted as collecting, but it wasn't the sort of collection you shared with anyone.

Baseball cards, I told him. As a kid.

In my spare time at work I continued reporting. I called Holden's boss at the data-imaging company, who told me that he did his best to accommodate Peter Holden's urge to go out of his way on his business travels and collect the McDonald's experience.

If you can handle his mysterious routes from point A to point B, he said, he's the best employee you could have.

I called Holden's ex-girlfriend. She told me that at first she couldn't understand why Holden stopped so often for snacks on their vacations, always at McDonald's. After about a year, she said, I finally confronted him. Why stop at McDonald's six times a day? Why not Burger King? I wasn't hungry or thirsty, so I'd sit in the car. I'd see him inside taking notes. I'm a psychotherapist, and I could never figure him out.

She went on record that McDonald's played no role in their eventual breakup.

I called officials at McDonald's corporate headquarters, who declined to comment. I called a woman at McClip, the barbershop inside the McDonald's headquarters building, where Holden told me he'd had his hair cut several times.

The stylist remembered him immediately. She said Holden was enamored of the fact of getting his hair cut in the same chair where the McDonald's CEO got his trim. In fact, once every six or eight weeks for nearly two years in the early 1990s, Peter Holden had made the 725-mile trip from his home in Virginia to Oak Brook, Illinois, to get a twelve-dollar haircut.

Thus did I come to write my first story for the *Wall Street Journal*, a front-pager, an A-hed, a humorous and lighthearted tale of one man's obsession that would turn out to represent the crowning achievement of my career in journalism, though I couldn't have known it at the time. The headline read:

Not All McDonald's Are Carbon Copies, a Collector Attests:
Peter Holden Eats at 10,893 and, Like a Wine Lover, Enjoys
Subtle Differences

That day the recipients of my fax deliveries, some of whom had yet to acknowledge my existence, dared to make eye contact. Some even whispered words of encouragement. It felt like my coming-out party, minus most of the things that make a party a party. Just before lunch, my telephone rang. It was a literary agent. He asked if I'd considered turning my story into a book. I told him I was flattered by the idea but I thought it wouldn't make much of a book. There were some details I wished I could have added if I'd had more space, but not many.

The agent said I was probably right. Maybe the thing to do, he said, is find ten other obsessed people and write stories about them and package them in a book of short pieces.

Maybe, I said.

The week after my story about Holden appeared, an assistant managing editor stopped by my desk and told me that he hoped to see more of my byline in the paper. Since my phone wasn't ringing with more good tips, I became the guy to whom editors turned when they needed someone to write a small item on deadline. I wrote one, for instance, about a medical study on the dangers of cigar smoking. The headline read: "Cigar Smokers Face Increased Risk of Cancer, Study Says." I thought this was pretty obvious, but the medical editor assured me it was breaking news.

After my first few months on the job, Francine Schwadel called me into her office and gave me a performance review. She said I did a very fine job of handing out faxes and was proving myself to be a diligent reporter. If I showed patience, I would one day be promoted and could move on to something more important than handing out faxes.

For a moment I was taken with the thought of someone bringing faxes to me.

I finished the term of my sublet, rented a moving van, and moved what little I owned in one trip to Bed-Stuy. To celebrate, I went for a few beers and a burger at McHale's, my farewell visit as a resident of the neighborhood, though I knew I'd always return, no matter where I lived in the city.

Three hours later, feeling a little queasy, I decided to splurge on a taxi home.

Where to? the driver said.

When I told him the address, he said, Where's that?

Bed-Stuy.

He looked at me in the mirror.

I think I can find it.

I hope so, I said. I've only been there twice.

He scribbled on his clipboard, reset the meter. A few moments later, stopped at a red light, he looked at me in the mirror again.

You know someone there?

I don't know anyone there. I just moved there this afternoon.

What for? The price?

Two bedrooms for eight hundred bucks.

Sweet deal, he said. But you're aware that ain't your neighborhood.

He was one of the few white-ethnic cabbies I'd seen in the city—Irish, apparently, from the name on the license on the back of his seat—but even so the sternness of his tone surprised me.

Yeah, haven't seen too many pale faces in the neighborhood, I said.

You're not going to, he said.

We drove in silence over the East River, the diorama of the city skyline receding behind us. He found the address without trouble.

Remember this, he said, turning to face me. When you

need a lift, tell your driver to use the Williamsburg Bridge. It's the quickest and easiest way. You come onto Broadway and look for Woodhull. Right after the hospital hang a right and you're on Marcus Garvey. Five minutes and you're home.

Thanks, appreciate that, I said.

Let me tell you something else, he said. A lot of drivers won't want to come out here. It's a no-man's-land for getting a fare back to the city. Watch how many taxis you see in the street. I'm telling you there won't be many. Easiest way to shirk a fare is to say, I don't know how to get there. So you'd better know for them.

Until then I hadn't felt the tiniest tremor of fear about my move. To be afraid, I thought, would have been to admit to a streak of latent racism, and I didn't believe I was racist. Nonetheless a veil of suspicion dropped between me and the neighborhood all of a sudden. Worried, I cast about for points in my favor, as if polishing my make-believe résumé of racial sensitivity. At the age of seventeen I'd read *The Autobiography of Malcolm X* and was so moved I went out and bought a T-shirt with his face silk-screened on the front. In Minneapolis, in 1992, I'd marched alongside some deodorant-averse white people to protest the verdict in the beating of Rodney King. In college I'd judged Martin Luther King, Jr.'s "I Have a Dream" speech the greatest of American orations. As a result of my liberal arts education, I'd gained some acquaintance with the works of Frederick Douglass, Langston Hughes, James Baldwin, Toni Morrison, names unknown in the house where I'd grown up. I owned several dozen jazz albums, from King Oliver to Sonny Rollins. In the greatest NBA rivalry of my lifetime I'd been on the side of the Lakers over the Celtics—Magic trumping Bird, Showtime all the way. Maybe this collection of random facts would cohere into a signal of my harmlessness and emanate from my being on the streets, discernible via ESP on the lower frequencies. Surely my new neighbors would recognize a kindred soul, a fellow American acquainted with the deep meaning of the blues. Class kinship would trump racial difference, that old dream of the democratic socialists.

Then again, the way the cabbie spoke, with a note of warning in his voice—as if he'd sniffed the provinces on me and felt compelled to protect me from my ignorance—clued me in to the fact that my choice of neighborhood was unlikely to be viewed by its longtime residents as a compensatory counterweight to the fact of my employment at the flagship paper of Dow Jones & Company, unless I wore a sandwich board announcing my motives on my walks to and from the subway. My family and friends were bemused that someone of my political persuasion would end up working at the *Wall Street Journal*, and the few colleagues at the paper with whom I shared the news of my new residence were just as baffled that I would choose to live someplace where I so obviously did not belong. At the newspaper the mere mention of whose name evoked images of power, I had none; in a neighborhood that stood as a stark example of powerlessness, I had the look of a man with more power than anyone by far. Walking down Marcus Garvey Boulevard each morning to the train, wearing a suit and tie on my journey between these worlds, I felt myself traversing the righteous path of the outcast. It was a kind of performance, a daily tightrope walk across a yawning chasm, a journey both precarious and surreal, and I savored every delicious and delirious second of it.

Once I convinced myself I would be welcomed in Bed-Stuy, it was only a short leap to imagine myself *saved* in Bed-Stuy. By being called to the surface of things, by being forced to rise out of self-obsession and deal with the tangible world around me as something other than a bad joke, maybe I could begin the work of forgetting the phone calls I hadn't made, the words I hadn't said. Maybe, by some miraculous encounter in the streets, I'd be granted the forgiveness I couldn't grant myself—or, failing that, endure my punishment and emerge reborn.

White Boy

onroe Street marked the northern edge of those stately brownstones that gave Bed-Stuy its architectural charm. Not just Monroe Street, but my *side* of Monroe Street. Across the street to the north most of the houses were wooden or vinyl-sided, and some had been abandoned, plywood nailed over their windows. A little farther north the Marcy Houses loomed, aesthetic monstrosities that always put me in mind of medium-security prison architecture, but taller. Jay Z had grown up there, but at the time I couldn't have told you the first thing about Jay Z, even though "Hard Knock Life (Ghetto Anthem)" had been playing all over the city for a year.

There were three businesses on the corner of Monroe and Marcus Garvey: the Fried Chicken Palace, a Chinese take-out, and a tiny bodega. Up the avenue, just before the projects, was the only grocery store within walking distance. I shopped there twice, once in ignorance and a second time in desperation. The fruits and vegetables looked secondhand. A box of macaroni and cheese sold for about twice what it would've cost on the Upper East Side of Manhattan. The neighborhood, it turned out, was what sociologists called a food desert.

One night I went to the Chinese takeout. The kitchen was sealed behind a wall of bulletproof glass so opaque that only the smells of food and fryer oil gave away the fact that the men in back, barely visible as white blurs, were cooking and not stamping license plates. I ordered the chicken lo mein and stood back to wait. Loitering was not encouraged. There was no place to sit. If you wanted to eat on the premises you could set your food on a chest-high shelf along the wall.

A man said to me, Hey, I saw you the other day.

He was short—maybe five-five—and wore thick glasses. The skin on his face was mottled pink in places, as if he'd had a series of skin grafts that hadn't quite worked out.

In the bodega across the street, I said.

What are you doing here?

Getting dinner.

No, I mean *here*, he said, waving his arm to take in the whole neighborhood.

I live here.

You buy a house?

I rent.

He stared at me with a look of profound confusion. He opened his mouth as if to speak but couldn't find the words.

A friend of mine put me in touch with the landlord, I said. He wanted to rent to people he knew, or people his friends knew. And the price was right. My name's Phil—I extended my hand—what's yours?

He told me and said, I been in the neighborhood forty-six years. Born and raised.

I'm a short-timer by comparison.

What do you do?

There were five or six people standing around waiting for food, and they were all looking at me. I tried to think of something to say—other than the truth—but nothing clever came to mind.

I work at the *Wall Street Journal*, I said.

Shit, he said. Trading stocks and making stacks of cash.

No, I said—and here I did lie, for reasons that were inexplicable; the lie just came to my lips and escaped in an instant—I write about people who trade stocks.

A journalist? he said. A *journalist*? He squinted and turned up his nose. Throwing mud at people, he said. Draggin' 'em through the dirt. Ruinin' people's right to make a living. A *journalist*. He turned and spat on the floor as if the word had dirtied his mouth.

I'd written five or six pieces in my time at the paper, most of them tiny spot-news fillers, things I could tap out at the margins of my days. I was still first and foremost a fax boy, earning barely twenty grand a year, but I was making myself sound like some kind of big shot. Still, I knew I couldn't backtrack without looking like a fool.

I throw mud at people who deserve mud flung at them, I said.

He smiled and looked around the room. He raised his arm and gestured toward me. I thought he might be about to hit me, and my arms tensed, ready to deflect his punch.

Instead he said, as if he were the arbiter of such things, as if he knew he held my fate in his hands but decided to let me slide: *This guy's all right.*

The woman behind the bulletproof glass called out my order. I stepped up and paid through the little cash-exchange hole. He sidled up as I put the change in my wallet.

Will you give me a dollar, man?

Give you a dollar?

Yeah, man, just a dollar.

Again I felt myself performing, everyone waiting to see what I'd say. I thought I'd do well to avoid establishing a reputation as the white boy in the neighborhood who went around giving away his money.

No, man, I worked hard for this dollar.

Come on, man.

I need this dollar. I need to buy lunch tomorrow. I need to pay my rent.

Okay, okay, he said, palms up in a gesture of surrender.

I'll see you around, though, I said.

That's right you will, he said. Every day.

I never saw him again.

Less than a year into my tenure at the *Journal,* I learned of a job opening on the Leisure & Arts page. It was listed on the company's internal Web site, a copyediting job, repairing split infinitives and run-on sentences. I fastened with unreasoning hope on the notion that the job—and the raise that came with it—could be mine.

My hope vanished the moment I learned that, in order to get the job, I would first have to sit for an interview with Bob Bartley, the editorial page editor of the paper, who oversaw hiring for the Leisure & Arts page, which he otherwise supervised with benign neglect. Bob Bartley was among the most influential American journalists of the second half of the twentieth century, although his name was not widely known outside of New York and Washington. He was fairly soft-spoken, and his posture was not what you'd call ideal. He rarely smiled, but when he did he looked like a cat who'd just swallowed your canary.

Bob Bartley's two abiding obsessions were taxes and weapons. He thought taxes should be cut always and everywhere, except for poor people, on whom they should be raised as a disincentive to being poor, and as for weapons he thought America should build as many as possible. The more weapons we had, in his view, the less likely we were to need them. But he believed that occasionally we needed them to bomb other nations that were trying to develop them too, because those nations couldn't be trusted not to use them. In order to further thwart the nations that, unlike ours, couldn't be trusted not to use their weapons, he thought we should spend however many trillions it took to build a missile-defense shield, that sci-fi umbrella that would protect America from the rain of other nations' missiles. Bob Bartley believed that with tax cuts, lots of weapons, and a missile-defense shield, Americans would remain safe, happy, and prosperous.

Bob Bartley had been writing editorials about these ideas for almost thirty years.

Someone once made a joke about editorial writers. Why is writing an editorial like pissing yourself in a blue serge suit? Because it gives you a warm feeling, and nobody notices what you've done.

Bob Bartley was no trouser-wetter, though. From what I could discern he never had warm feelings, and people in power tended to notice what he wrote.

The arena in which he'd had his greatest influence was tax policy. He was American journalism's leading proponent of trickle-down economics: by cutting taxes on rich people and raising them for poor people, he argued, more money would end up not only in the hands of rich people but—because the rich people would spend it on housekeepers and yachts—in the hands of people who kept houses and built fancy boats. Because everyone would be making more money, the government would generate more revenue in taxes, even though the top tax rates were lower. Since bloating government coffers with more taxpayer money was actually a *bad* thing, an evil outcome of sound policy, the government would be obliged to funnel the extra tax revenues to bomb-building projects—in effect throwing the money away, since it created wealth, in the form of weapons, that could only be used once, if at all, and then only to destroy, never to create more wealth, which thus ran counter to the essence of capitalism, wealth creating wealth—while at the same time cutting programs for poor people and generally running the machinery of government with an incompetence bordering on malice, which would make poor people angry at the government and entice them to vote for

Republicans, just like most rich people did, ensuring Republican rule forever.

Despite the baroque strangeness of some of his ideas, Bob Bartley had once won a Pulitzer Prize.

When I first joined the paper, Bob Bartley was in the late, hysterical stages of his obsession with Bill Clinton. Bob Bartley's editorial page had printed enough editorials about Whitewater to fill three thousand pages in six anthologies. Bob Bartley was proud of these books, even though no one bought them. He thought Whitewater was comparable to Watergate; he was hoping to bring down a president, in the manner of Woodward and Bernstein, and perhaps win another Pulitzer Prize. But despite his three thousand pages of editorials, the Whitewater investigation devolved into an absurd argument about whether fellatio is actually sex, and the president did not resign and was not forced from office, although Bob Bartley was adamant that he should have been, because Bob Bartley did not approve of extramarital fellatio, at least not for Democrats. When a reporter had asked him whether he and his editorial page would've attacked Newt Gingrich or another prominent Republican faced with similar charges of sexual misconduct, Bob Bartley admitted that "we would have defended them. That's the way it is."

I was nervous when I went to Bob Bartley's office. My internship at the *Nation* featured prominently on my résumé. While the work I had done there was utterly harmless to the spread of corporate capitalism, the *Nation* was known to say kind things about socialists. Bob Bartley detested socialists.

Bob Bartley held my résumé in his hands. I feared he would ask me about socialism, taxes, trickle-down economics. I would then face a choice: I could either tell him what I thought about these things, whereupon he would refuse to hire me to work on the Leisure & Arts page, or I could betray my principles, such as they were, and lie. I'd been here before, and I knew which path I'd choose.

He did not ask me about these things. We talked about Minnesota and Iowa, where, it turned out, we had both lived as boys. He'd been born in southwest Minnesota but grew up mostly in Ames, Iowa, while I'd been born in Ames, Iowa, and grew up mostly in southwest Minnesota. This struck me as appropriate, our moving in opposite directions at the beginning of our lives—me upward and to the left on the map, him downward and to the right.

Bob Bartley asked me only one serious question, with two leading follow-ups: What is your ambition in life? Do you, for instance, want to be a reporter? Or do you want to be editorial page editor of the *Wall Street Journal*?

I was pretty sure I didn't want to be a reporter, especially not at the *Wall Street Journal*, where many reporters covered a single industry (airlines, pharmaceuticals) or even a single company (General Motors, Microsoft), had minimal opportunities to afflict the comfortable and even fewer to comfort the afflicted, and never detached themselves from their cell phones. Even though a part of me did want to be editorial page editor of the *Wall Street Journal*, which was the same thing as saying I wanted to be the most important person at the world's most important publication, I knew

I'd never get that chance, because I didn't believe any of the things Bob Bartley believed. I figured I'd have to say something completely harmless, though not without a hint of some trivial ambition.

I said, No, I want to write historical fiction.

My answer pleased him, as I'd figured it would. It wasn't long before I was told the job was mine.

When I moved to the Leisure & Arts page, I assumed I'd have no personal contact with the editorial writers, but my cubicle was situated smack in the midst of theirs. A couple of them came forward to welcome me, but most of them did not. The ones who welcomed me overlooked the fact that my politics were repugnant. Those who did not welcome me could not overlook that fact. Admittedly, by hanging posters of Emma Goldman and Ralph Nader in my cubicle, I made it a hard fact to overlook.

Though I had little in the way of social interaction with the editorial writers, I began to read their pieces very closely, sometimes even dipping into the archives to sample their obsessions over the decades. They wrote with the zeal of converts, as if they'd all been communists in their youth, and each of them rode a favorite right-wing hobbyhorse into the ground, month after month, year after year: not only cutting taxes and stockpiling weapons but the treachery and moral lassitude of the Palestinians, the deleterious effects of the 1960s on American moral values, the heroic necessity of Pinochet's bloody dictatorship in crushing democratic socialism in Chile. The collective voice of the newspaper—the unsigned editorial—was always the furthest to the right of the range of beliefs held by the editorial board members, no accident on Bob Bartley's part. He held the most extreme position on almost every issue and, because he couldn't write three editorials a day himself, took great care in his choice of lieutenants. His fondness for partisan hacks led him to hire people who could just as well have been Republican speechwriters, as indeed some of them had been (Peggy Noonan) or soon would be (Bill McGurn).

For the most part, Bob Bartley held meetings only with people who shared his opinions, in a little conference room near my cubicle—meetings with men like Kenneth Starr, the special prosecutor who wrote the most famous volume of pornography during the 1990s, and William Bennett, the moralist who gambled away, at the tables in Vegas, the earnings from his books and speeches, which proselytized on behalf of virtue and self-discipline. I came to think of this conference room as the echo chamber for the vast right-wing conspiracy, though not because of its acoustics.

I tried once to engage in a reasonable discussion about politics with one of the editorial writers. She was a voluble young woman who'd grown up in Oregon and gone to college at Princeton. She worked in the cubicle next to mine, so I overheard her on the phone every day, talking the crazy with like-minded crazies—suggesting, for instance, that the U.S. Navy, after being pressured to stop raining practice bombs on the Puerto Rican island of Vieques, should instead bombard the Arctic National Wildlife Refuge, making it the opposite of a wildlife refuge. She cackled when she said this, though not because she was kidding.

She wrote a lot about the environment—she was reliably against it—and one time I told her I disagreed with something she'd written about federal forest policy. The essence of my argument was simple: I didn't think trees should be cut down carelessly. She told me that trees existed to be cut down. She said she preferred clear-cuts—forests transformed into nonforests. She said clear-cuts grew back as peaceful meadows, which were aesthetically superior to forests. I disagreed not just on the aesthetics but also in regards to the effect on wildlife and watersheds. She said I had an unhealthy, sentimental attitude about trees; she accused me of wanting to hug them. I told her I didn't want to hug them, I just didn't think they should all die and take with them songbirds and squirrels and all the other life that make an ancient forest more than a stand of timber poised to become lumber. She said most trees would be better off dead, after which they could be given a more useful second life as furniture, houses, or fax paper.

We didn't talk much after that, although we always exchanged cordial hellos when passing in the hallways.

It took me a while to notice that the only people who would speak to me on the streets of Bed-Stuy were over forty or strung out on crack. No twenty-five-year-old guy was going to strike up a casual conversation with a white dude in plain view of anyone else; even less likely a young woman. The women were magisterial in their ability to pretend I wasn't there when we passed in the streets. I loved the irony of my status as an invisible man. The homeboys would cast a glance my way—surprised, bemused, sometimes aggressive, as if sizing me up, trying to guess my angle—but not the women. To them I was less than an ectoplasm, though I know they sensed my presence and must have been curious. I couldn't blame them for their posture of indifference. In fact I was secretly grateful. They didn't need any trouble, and neither did I.

For a while I lived without a home telephone, so I made my calls at a pay phone, around the corner on Marcus Garvey. One afternoon I left a message for a friend I planned to meet that night for dinner. I hung up and turned to find myself in sole possession of the gaze of a woman maybe fifty years old, wearing a green and gold head scarf. She walked with an erectness of posture that made me think she might be some kind of neighborhood ambassador, there to take the measure of me.

Happy New Year, she said. You new to the neighborhood?

I live on Monroe Street, I said. Just moved in.

Well, welcome. You know, there's another couple in the neighborhood. I saw them in the Laundromat a few weeks ago. Young folks like you.

I hadn't seen a white face yet. The closest I had come were rumors, secondhand reports of sightings, which sort of disappointed me. I wanted the other thirteen to have fled. I wanted to be the one and only.

72

I'm sorry, she said. That was a foolish thing to say. You know what I mean, I hope.

You mean about the other couple?

She nodded, looking rueful.

Of course, I said. It's pretty obvious.

Well, kinda put my foot in my mouth.

There's no point denying I'm white. It's a hard thing not to notice.

It felt good to speak frankly, as if by stating the irrefutable I was doing my part to advance the cause of racial understanding.

This neighborhood is ninety-nine percent black, she said. When you see white folk here they catch your attention, like that couple I told you about. They had dreadlocks and all these tattoos. Real eccentric-looking, but nice.

When I'd tried to imagine the other thirteen white people, that's what I typically pictured—white Rastafarians, that most peculiar of oxymorons.

I know what it's like to stick out in a neighborhood, she said. The other day I went out for a typewriter ribbon. It was Hanukkah, so all the Jewish stores were closed. I didn't realize it was a Jewish holiday until I found a couple of stores locked. So I went back home and looked in the yellow pages and called some other places. I found one that had the ribbon I needed. Except it was in Greenpoint. I had to take the bus, and after I got off the bus I was lost. I went into a bar to ask for directions. The place was filled with old white men, Polish or Irish or something. What nationality are your people?

French and Irish, I said.

May the road rise up to meet you. That's Irish. I'm African and Hispanic. Anyway, I'm in this bar with a dozen old white men, somewhere in Greenpoint.

Looking pretty scary half drunk in the afternoon, I said. Oh, yes.

I know. I've been in those bars.

You got that right, darlin'. I told the bartender I was lost. He looked at me a little funny but he took me outside and pointed down the street and showed me where to go. He was pretty sweet about it. In the end we're all human no matter our color. We live in our neighborhoods but we're all in this together. The border of the world ain't the edge of our neighborhood.

I'm finding it instructive to live somewhere where I'm conscious of my skin color, I said. I've never had that experience. What you find first are the kindness and curiosity of strangers. At least here.

Most places, she said, most places.

It seemed as if we'd sussed out an essential truth about the human condition, and there was nothing left to say.

I should run, she said. I've kept you long enough.

Happy New Year, I said. Maybe I'll see you around.

Indeed you will, she said. Keep faith with the Lord and all will be well.

I never saw her again.

I worked ten to six on weekdays, so I was usually around the neighborhood only at night. Young people flirted outside the

Fried Chicken Palace. Deals went down on Marcus Garvey. The heat in my apartment was oppressive that winter, the steam radiators working full bore without modulation, so I left my bedroom windows open. Lying in bed reading by lamplight, I could hear the night sounds below: a shout in the street, the thump of a bass line from a passing car. Most of the time these sounds were a comfort to me, evidence of a complicated social life I could access vicariously. I knew I'd never be a real part of the community, but that didn't matter. I wanted a situation where nothing was asked of me, nothing expected, and while you could find that pretty much anywhere in New York if you were a refugee from the hinterlands, it seemed purer for me in Bed-Stuy. At night I would often see groups of men my age gathered in the barbershops, cutting each other's hair and laughing, dapping, telling jokes. There was no way in hell I could have joined them, I knew that, but I didn't mind. Scenes of joy in camaraderie only reinforced the bitter bite of my bittersweet solitude.

I devoted my free hours to reading, as I mostly had since my brother's death, reading being one of the surest escapes from the cocoon of solipsism in which I was otherwise so comfortably nestled. One book in particular seized me that winter: James Baldwin's collected nonfiction, *The Price of the Ticket.* I'd read parts of it years earlier, and now I picked it up again, looking, I suppose, to his fierce intelligence for an anchor in the swirl of impressions I'd encountered in Bed-Stuy. Instead the thing that gripped me to the point of obsession was a passage from the essay "Nothing Personal," which a footnote said was "written with Richard Avedon" but sounded like vintage Baldwin:

> . . . sometimes, at 4 a.m. . . . with all one's wounds awake and throbbing, and all one's ghastly inadequacy staring and shouting from the walls and the floor—the entire universe having shrunk to the prison of the self—death glows like the only light on a high, dark, mountain road, where one has, forever and forever! lost one's way.—And many of us perish then.
>
> But if one can reach back, reach down—into oneself, into one's life—and find there some witness, however unexpected or ambivalent, to one's reality, one will be enabled, though perhaps not very spiritedly, to face another day. . . . What one must be enabled to recognize, at four o'clock in the morning, is that one has no right, at least not for reasons of private anguish, to take one's life. All lives are connected to other lives and when one man goes, much more than the man goes with him.

I'd done some systematic reading in the literature of suicide, most of it amounting to a thumbs-up or -down on whether it was permissible. That question held little interest for me. No matter what judgment Kant or Schopenhauer offered on the subject, thirty thousand Americans a year did themselves in, hundreds of thousands more worldwide. I intuited the raw impulsiveness of the act. You either got there or you didn't; the route was mysterious, and no religious prohibition or philosophical text seemed likely to sway a person in the throes of suicidal despair. Who has time for *The Myth of Sisyphus* when the gun is right there within reach? ("There is but one truly serious philosophical problem," Camus had written. "Judging whether life is or is not worth living amounts to answering the fundamental question of philosophy.") Anyway, in the case of my brother, the deed had been done. It hardly mattered whether I condemned him or offered my posthumous blessing. He was dead and he was going to stay dead, no need to bury him at the crossroads with a stake in his heart.

Baldwin had a point of view on the morality of the deed, but even as he made his judgment he expressed a nuanced sympathy for the lost and the damned. He saw that dark night through their eyes. To find my brother's state of mind—my own state of mind many nights—expressed so clearly offered me a different sort of anchor than the one I'd been looking for. I repeated that one ringing line to myself—*all lives are connected to other lives and when one man goes, much more than the man goes with him*—so often that it became a mantra, a reason for living another day. It gripped me so fixedly I ignored a pertinent warning that came not long after:

> Then one selects the uniform which one will wear. This uniform is designed to telegraph to others what to see so they will not be made uncomfortable and probably hostile by being forced to look on another human being. . . . It is necessary to make anyone on the streets think twice before attempting to vent his despair on you.

....

Before I moved to Bed-Stuy, I'd been under the impression that the crack epidemic—always so called, as if it were some virus beyond human agency, akin to Ebola or monkey pox—had run its course in the city. There were no longer any stories about it in the papers, but every other day or so, on my walks to and from the subway, I'd find an empty vial in the seams of the sidewalks. Their stoppers came in various colors, and soon I had a little collection—yellow, red, white, purple, green, blue. In the mornings before work, when I'd try to write and fail, I'd pull them out of my desk drawer and hold them in the palm of my hand, wondering what it felt like to have that kind of high, that kind of need for a high. Out in the streets you could see the crackheads coming from a block away: stumbling, weaving, a beatific smile on their faces if they'd just smoked up, their eyes meat-red and their noses smeared with snot. If you got close enough they smelled something horrible, like they were already dead and beginning to rot.

There was a woman who hung around the bodega on the corner asking everyone who passed for cash or beer. She may have been no older than twenty-five but she had only half her teeth left. The skin on her face was swollen so tight I feared it might rupture if she so much as coughed. Her shoes were sometimes mismatched. Other times she went barefoot. I could tell she'd once been a great beauty. She still had the legs, although they were awfully skinny now, and her eyes were huge and lit from within as if she'd seen the Rapture coming.

Mister, wooyoo bry me and ache bull? she slurred, the first time I saw her.

I'm sorry?

Mister, wooyoo priss doobie faber an bry me an ache bull?

It took me another moment to understand she was asking for a forty-ouncer of malt liquor.

My first impulse was to say, Honey, that wouldn't be doing you a favor. But what sort of favor could I do her? She terrified me, she'd ruined herself so completely—as if committing suicide in slow motion.

Do you smoke? I said, making the universal symbol for a cigarette, index finger and middle finger splayed in front of my lips. I didn't want her to think I meant crack.

She nodded.

In the bodega I bought a carton of orange juice, asked the clerk to throw in two loosies.

I handed the woman a cigarette, lit it for her, lit my own. Her hand shook as she held it. She thanked me, told me I was a nice man.

I thought: No, I'm not. I am not a nice man.

Instead I said: You're welcome.

As much as there was a part of me that secretly feared—and even more secretly craved—being harmed in Bed-Stuy, there was another cloistered and delusional part of me that thought I might be redeemed by intimacy with squalor and degradation. Those words appeared more than once in my journals around that time, and what was a better synonym for the squalid and degraded than a crackhead on the streets of Bed-Stuy? Despite the veneer of higher education, I was still an ignorant white boy. I'd never seen a Spike Lee movie, never listened to a word of Biggie Smalls, but I knew the motto *Bed-Stuy Do or Die*, and with no appreciation for the obvious irony I'd taken it as my own. I may have read Baldwin but I hadn't understood.

Mired as I was in my own dark trip, I wasn't terribly interested in the social texture of the neighborhood—in its history, in the stories of the people who lived there, their struggles and hopes, fears and dreams—and truth be told, I didn't want to get all that intimate with squalor and degradation, whatever they might mean. It's not like I was prepared to take a crackhead home and give her a hot bath and a home-cooked meal. I got a little tingle from being in proximity to self-inflicted suffering, but I didn't want to have to *do* anything about it. I constantly reminded myself that I hadn't gone to school to be a social worker. I'd chosen a course of study that taught me various tricks for how to observe the workings of the world, to take notes and write them up in stories, so I took notes, as much out of habit as anything. I knew I had zero chance of convincing an editor at the *Wall Street Journal* to let me write a feature on the myriad ways the American government and moneyed interests had turned their backs on Bed-Stuy, a neglect—a spiteful, willful neglect—that was nothing short of criminal.

For a time, squalor and degradation were all I could see

in the streets, or all I chose to see—and not just in the world around me but in my own mind. At my day job I could impersonate a competent, self-possessed young man, but my inner life festered with diseased visions:

At the laundromat today I saw a poster tacked to the wall. It said the 79th precinct's homicide squad is looking for information about the death of a livery cab driver who was found murdered in his car on the corner of Marcus Garvey Blvd. and Monroe St. on Feb. 1. The thought of it chilled me: a dead body forty steps from my front door, shot for the cash in his pocket.

On the stoop across the street a man lifted his shriveled penis from his pants and relieved himself on the topmost step. His urine steamed in the cold. It steamed in its arc and steamed where it splashed on the concrete.

Think of the cool reassurance of gunmetal in palm. The dull and languid hereafter, the painless hereafter. Think of the bliss of death.

I'd been in the neighborhood a couple of months when I was given a raise at work, and one of the ways I celebrated was by going on a little shopping spree at Century 21, just up the street from the paper. I bought a suit jacket off a sales rack, a DKNY number that fit well enough, though it was a touch long in the arms. On another sales rack I found a pair of pants that more or less matched the jacket. I bought three new dress shirts and four ties to go with them. To complete the ensemble, I rode the train up to Eighth Avenue and Forty-first Street, to a hat shop I'd passed many times on my walks through the city, and I bought myself a sharp-looking fedora, black, with a red and yellow feather in the band.

Most of the men at the paper wore white shirts and patterned ties that looked like they'd been bought a generation or two before. If you looked closely you could see little stains on them where they'd caught a splash of soup or a dribble of mustard, possibly during the Reagan administration. I opted for colored shirts—salmon-pink, lime-green, cornflower-blue—and ties with a bit of pizzazz in their patterns. The fedora, though, was the real flourish, a gesture of pure irony. It offered not a clue about who I really was, where I'd come from, what I believed.

A natty socialist at the *Wall Street Journal*. A white guy in a black neighborhood. Strange how comfortable my discomfort became.

In other words, I was asking for it.

The woman who was supposed to move from Detroit and share the apartment never did. After a while, another friend of Mary's became my roommate. Beth had just ended a long-term relationship with a woman and decided to explore the complications of hetero life by seeing a married man. Among the palest people I'd ever encountered, she was impossible not to notice on the streets of Bed-Stuy—she made me look swarthy by comparison—but she carried herself with an air of oblivious good cheer that made me believe she'd remain immune to trouble. She wasn't around much anyway. She stayed most nights with her boyfriend Dave in Manhattan, in the apartment he'd taken after leaving his wife.

Dave came to Bed-Stuy once to spend the night. I never saw him there again, but he told me a story I never forgot. He'd taken the train partway, then the bus. It was rush hour and the bus was full, so he'd had to stand. In front of him a woman held a child to her chest. The child couldn't stop staring over her mother's shoulder. Block after block the child stared, her eyes, according to Dave, revealing an intensity of awe unlike anything he'd ever seen.

I'm pretty sure the kid had never seen a white person, Dave said.

When the bus drew near Dave's stop, he scooted a couple of steps toward the door. Just before he got off, the little girl reached over her mother's shoulder and, in the most tentative way imaginable, touched Dave's cheek with her finger.

It was almost as if she couldn't believe I was real, Dave said. Once she realized my skin felt like anyone else's, you should have seen her smile.

As I walked the streets of the neighborhood that story kept returning to me. Not because anything so dramatic happened to me, but because I did feel the force of people's curiosity—the sideways glances I got as I walked the streets, the questions I fielded from the neighborhood elders while buying a carton of orange juice in a bodega. A lot of people

assumed I was a Jehovah's Witness peddling the literature
of salvation, since that was about the only kind of white person who made an appearance in the heart of Bed-Stuy, the
kind harvesting souls for Jesus. This was the funniest joke
I'd heard in months, all the funnier for its repetition, but I
didn't laugh for long.

One night I went to meet my uncle in Manhattan. He
was in the city on business from Seattle. He'd invited me to
dinner on a client's expense account, a seven-course affair at
a fancy TriBeCa restaurant, so I put on a new shirt and tie,
my new jacket, the fedora. I was strolling down the street
toward the C train, looking forward to an evening of food
and wine and talk, whistling to myself—I'd been listening to some Sinatra before I left, the famous live recording
with Count Basie, in particular "Fly Me to the Moon," that
swinging masterpiece—when I was jumped from behind.
I say jumped, but that doesn't do justice to the force of it.
I'm not sure if the guy meant to keep a grip on me or not.
He hit me so hard I flew about eight feet before I landed on
the sidewalk. It all happened so quickly, I suppose I acted
on pure adrenal reflex. I jumped up and ran. Halfway down
the block I stopped to catch my breath, having heard no
footsteps behind me. I'd lost my glasses and my hat, and my
knees and palms were scratched and bleeding. The rest of
me seemed intact, if severely jangled. I couldn't see very well
without my glasses but I did notice a man walking toward
me, lit from behind by a streetlamp, his face obscured in
shadow.

Mister, he said, your hat.

He held it in his outstretched hand.

I was still too stunned to speak, and there was something about him that made me nervous—perhaps the fact that he seemed more concerned about returning my hat than inquiring about my well-being. He said it three times—*Mister, your hat*—and held it in front of him in one hand, like a priest administering the Eucharist. I extended my hand to take it from him. Just as my fingertips touched the brim he yanked it away. I turned and ran toward the street. A tree and a parked car blocked my path, and in the half second it took me to change course, he jumped on my back. I carried him across the street in a piggyback ride before he wrestled me to the sidewalk.

Don't fucking move, he said. My friend's got a gun and he ain't afraid to use it.

I was on my hands and knees, gasping for breath, unable to see the guy on top of me, and I thought: *You think I give a shit, you fuckers? Go ahead. Go ahead and kill me.*

A pair of feet appeared in front of my face, spread in the posture of a man about to take target practice.

Hand over your wallet. And nothing stupid or you're gonna get hurt.

The guy on my back gave it to his friend, who emptied the cash—fifty bucks—and dropped the wallet on the ground.

Don't look up, don't follow us, and don't call the cops and we won't have to hunt your ass down and shoot you.

They ran down the street, laughing as they went.

I stood, testing my ankles and knees. I brushed myself off, flexing my elbows and fingers. I touched my lip, which was swollen and bleeding. I ran my tongue over my teeth and found them all still there, though I spat a mouthful of blood.

There was a car sitting in the street, idling, its lights on, its muffler sending little thought-balloon shapes of exhaust into the air, but when I went to its window I found it unoccupied. Up the street I went, hobbling a little, stooping to look for the shapes of my glasses, my hat—the hat my muggers had used like bait to hook some idiot fish by the mouth.

For a while afterward, my fear boiled up in plain view. I'd risen to the surface of things, all right, though not in the way I'd hoped—or perhaps exactly in the way I'd hoped. I was surprised by the vehemence of my outrage; I hadn't expected to feel so protective of my own skin. My sense of distinction in the neighborhood, my illusory belief in my own goodness and even bravery, it all vanished. Though I ought to have counted myself lucky—I'd merely suffered a few bruises, lost fifty bucks—I instead felt forewarned, as if the mugging were merely a teaser of what lay in store for me. It exposed a part of me I'd managed to avoid knowing was there, the run-of-the mill bigot, the guy who casts a jaundiced eye on a whole group of people for the actions of a couple of punks redistributing the wealth with the finesse of middle linebackers. It was sport, what they'd done. They'd wanted my money, and I must have looked like I had a lot more than it turned out I did.

For a week or so I imagined crossing the river to Jersey and getting my hands on a nine. I'd shove its snout into someone's ear, the next person who dared look at me crossways. I'd become the one to fear instead of the one who feared.

Emotion trumping intellect, problem-solving with guns: maybe they ran in the family.

It was just a few days later when the verdict came down in the murder of Amadou Diallo. Like many New Yorkers I'd been appalled by the poor man's fate: a West African immigrant street peddler, in the wrong place at the wrong time, shot by four members of a Street Crimes Unit in the Bronx as he fumbled for proof of ID. The officers had fired forty-one shots at Diallo as he stood in his apartment vestibule, holding in his hand nothing more threatening than a wallet—a black wallet the cops took for a gun. On February 25, 2000, a jury acquitted the cops of all wrongdoing. The news was loud and clear and not exactly breaking: the police could shoot an innocent man on the streets of New York and there would be no consequences. An innocent *black* man, that is. It was hard to imagine a similar verdict if the victim had been a white man in Manhattan.

On the day after the acquittal, walking through the city as I often did on weekend afternoons, I came upon a parade of protesters streaming down Broadway, chanting, *It's just a wallet, not a gun, no excuse for forty-one.* As with many public protests in the city, I agreed with the protesters on principle. Like them, I thought the verdict was a travesty. Unlike them, I didn't want to reduce my feelings about it to a refrain that stated the obvious in the form of a rhyme. I remembered, all too vividly, chanting, *No justice, no peace*, in the streets of Minneapolis in 1992, one of the emptiest slogans I'd ever uttered, as if I had any intention of continually disturbing the peace in the absence of justice for Rodney King or anyone else.

I watched them pass by and then I walked on.

Going home that night from the subway, I came upon four young men having an animated discussion outside a bodega on Marcus Garvey. When I passed within earshot I heard one of the men say, No, no, this is fucking *bullshit*, bro. It's time we fought back against these motherfuckers. I'm talking real firepower. We gotta send a message. They put a bullet in one of us, we put two in one of them. Forty-one for Diallo, eighty-two for *him*—and he pointed at me, thumb and forefinger at a right angle, in the shape of a gun.

I turned away and walked on.

A week later I saw a flyer announcing a gathering at Ebenezer Baptist Church, not far from my apartment. The Reverend Al Sharpton, it said, would be the keynote speaker. When the night came I polished my black dress shoes, donned my finest churchworthy threads, and went to see what the reverend had to say.

I took a seat in the balcony as the choir began to sway and sing. Just as I'd shed my coat and settled in, a man came to the end of my row, pointed at me, and said: I have a lady I'd like to seat there. Would you mind moving?

I looked around. There were numerous empty seats

nearby, seats closer to the aisle, but his tone insinuated that it didn't matter one bit if I minded. It was a little power trip, and I played my part. Who could blame him? Such chances must not have come his way often. I nodded, gathered my coat, and stepped away. For a while I moved through the church, looking for another place to sit. I decided I'd do best to stand in the back of the balcony. On my walk around the church I'd counted two other white faces out of perhaps three hundred—one carrying a TV news camera, the other a microphone.

The program began with half an hour of gospel music from a choir dressed in blue and gold robes. The entire congregation stood and sang and clapped. The energy was electric, contagious, like nothing I'd experienced—certainly not in the dour Catholic services of my youth, with their mournful hymns, their repeated messages of inexpungable guilt. At that moment, swept up by a communal energy for the first time in a long time, I felt prepared to give something of myself. I wanted to be asked to do something useful, something brave in the service of justice. I didn't know what the something was but I knew I'd be ready if I heard it. I'd spent too much time thinking about a subject that scrambled all categories of justice, and I was growing sick of my befuddlement. I wanted answers.

The likelihood of my hearing them seemed to diminish noticeably when the first speaker welcomed us to "reservation headquarters," by which metaphor I would have been a visiting agent of the Bureau of Indian Affairs.

The Reverend Sharpton spoke last. In high biblical

cadence he sketched a series of proposals to rectify the injustice of the Diallo killing. When you go to the polls on Tuesday for the presidential primary, he said, reject the corrupt status quo and write in the name *Diallo*. We want to have thousands, tens of thousands, *hundreds* of thousands of votes for Amadou Diallo. We want to show the powers that be that this city will not move on until justice is served!

When someone asks you how you are, he said, you reply: *Amadou*. Let his name ring from our lips daily, hourly, on every street corner in the city! Let me hear you say it—Amadou!

Amadou.

Amadou!

Amadou.

He continued with a proposal to cripple the city's financial institutions by withdrawing black money from white banks. Then he closed with a retelling of the biblical story of David, which he linked to his own interactions with Diallo's father.

I told him, he said, I told him that in spite of my funny suit and the fact that I'm a Christian and you're a Muslim, we are brothers, separated long ago on the continent of Africa!

The reverend's sermon was a slightly better plan for fighting racial injustice than the one I'd heard on the street: trade two bullets for one. Then again, in that plan I'd have served some purpose, a nice white target in the dark. My money wasn't black. My money was green, and it was clearly safer in the bank than on my person. If I started going around muttering *Amadou*, I'd have been seen as a danger to myself or others. I'd been a fool to think I was among the reverend's audience just because I was in the reverend's audience.

As the music wound down afterward, I made my way toward the exit. Out of the corner of my eye I saw a familiar face—my landlord, Ben, the suave Trinidadian. I sliced sideways through the crowd, placed a hand on his shoulder.

Ben, I said. Good to see you.

I'm not sure what I expected—perhaps a little friendly chitchat, an exchange of impressions on what we'd just witnessed. I thought he'd at least acknowledge me, the gay-friendly dude who paid his rent on time. But he must have seen a whole mess of trouble he didn't need, because he recoiled slightly, as if he didn't know me.

I stood there dumbly, a pariah. In a moment he was gone, lost in the crowd.

Walking home along Fulton Street, then north on Malcolm X Boulevard, I knew my time in Bed-Stuy was up, and that it must have looked to the outside observer like nothing more than an exercise in cheap voyeurism—slumming, quite literally. To say out loud that I knew a thing or two about the emotional devastation wrought by gun violence: How far would that have gotten me? About the only commonality in the stories of Diallo and my brother was that white hands had held the guns.

When I knocked at Ben's apartment the next week, he didn't answer. I slipped a note under the door, giving him notice that I'd be gone by the end of the month.

I never saw him again.

Lover Boy

My new boss, Raymond Sokolov, was the sophisticate among my immediate colleagues at the *Journal*. In 1982 he'd founded the Leisure & Arts page as a daily staple of the paper. Prior to that he'd been a book and movie critic for *Newsweek*, a food editor at the *New York Times*, and a columnist for *Natural History* magazine. He'd written several books, among them a biography of A. J. Liebling. With his diminutive stature, his shock of white hair, his round spectacles and colorful bow ties, he had the appearance of a mischievous, throwback intellectual, a holdover from the glory days of *PM* and the *Herald-Tribune*. He was no ideologue when it came to politics. He seemed, from what I could gather in our oblique conversations, to be a sensible moderate—except on Israel, where he may have been to the right of Bob Bartley—but he had a streak of iconoclasm, a desire to tweak the sensibilities of the powers that were, which gave him a raffish charm. Working for him was a pleasure, as long as you didn't screw up. Once he'd read a piece, he washed his hands of it and preferred not to think of it again. Negotiating his changes with writers could be tricky when they didn't approve. I quickly learned that was my problem, not his. He left his subordinates alone to their work, and his trust made me want to do it justice.

Copyediting is peculiar work, a realm for word geeks and control freaks, part art and part science, and ultimately an exercise in professional anonymity. It's not as if readers have the chance to compare a writer's first draft with the printed version—look how much was needed!—so my work went completely unnoticed until a mistake showed up in print. The better I did my job, the more I receded into obscurity, even from Ray, so that I came to understand the ultimate goal was an erasure of my existence beyond interactions with the writers whose work I smoothed over, and the people in production who brought it all together in the end. Copy editors were the Zamboni drivers of the newspaper world. We kept the surface polished so the writers could perform their little pirouettes.

In the course of editing Ray's stable of critics, I played both cheerleader and scold in varying ratios as needed. I spoke by phone with interesting characters on at least a weekly basis: Nat Hentoff, the *Village Voice* columnist who wrote about jazz and was a living link to some of its legendary players; Ada Louise Huxtable, one of the most regal beings on the planet and America's preeminent architecture critic during the second half of the twentieth century; and the novelist Francine Prose, who wrote fluently about art and never failed to answer her phone in a breathless rush, as if juggling five assignments at once.

But the writer whose work changed my life came out of

nowhere. Late in 1999, Ray came up with an idea to get a friend of his, the poet Frederick Seidel, the exposure Ray thought he deserved. I'd never heard of Seidel; Ray said he was brilliant but had a tough time getting started on a poem. In fact, in a review in the *Journal* in the late 1980s, which I found by searching the online archives, Ray had called him "gifted" but "maddeningly unproductive." Seventeen years had passed between his first collection of poems and his second. In a career spanning forty years, he was about to publish his fifth book. Ray's plan was to give Seidel a monthly deadline, as if he were a columnist. Seidel would write one poem per month under the title of that month, and not only would the deadline prod him to action, the paper would offer him a readership the size of which most poets could only dream.

Here, Ray said one day, reaching into his bookshelves. Take these home with you. See what you think.

I spent that evening in the bathtub with four of Seidel's collections. Some of what I found was beautiful, sweet little rhapsodies in staccato lines, but reading him more often felt like riding shotgun on a fancy motorbike, through a city of voluptuous corruption as imagined by Hieronymus Bosch, with a mad driver tricked out in handmade shoes and Savile Row finery. The voice of the poems was absolutely shameless, musical and brutal in equal measure. He was a dandy, a daredevil, a scourge of official pieties, a celebrant of luxury, unsentimental in the extreme, sometimes innocent, more often guilty. He wrote with a bracing mix of erotic derangement and total liberty, and the images that recurred—cockpit voice recorders, women in stockings and

garters—were charged with morbid mystery or an amo-
rous aura or sometimes both. Among his obsessions was the
thought of suicide, and I found new lines to add to my collection of commonplace quotes. *Children, of all things bad,
the best is to kill a king. / Next best: to kill yourself out of
fear of death....* He had a knack for asking the sort of question I thought I'd been alone in asking:

> If you put a gun to your temple and close your eyes,
> And the enormous pressure builds and builds,
> And slowly you squeeze the trigger . . .
> Do you hear the big bang?

The dude knew. He'd found words for a subject too often
taboo. Sitting in the tub as the water turned tepid, growing
excited at the many moments of recognition, I came upon
a line to which I had a physical reaction, as if my skin had
been pricked by a pin: *Convinced life is meaningless, / I
lack the courage of my conviction.*

Seidel began to write his newspaper poems in March
2000, and it was my job to format them, make sure all the
italics and em-dashes and capital letters were just so, and
then fax him a copy to inspect and approve. I was too shy
to tell him his earlier poems had hit me with such force. I
didn't want to sound like what I feared I was, the kind of
guy who reads poetry in search of himself. When we talked
on the phone, I felt like a supplicant in the presence of royalty. Here was a man who as a freshman at Harvard had
visited Ezra Pound in the hospital and had the temerity

to suggest corrections to Pound's translation of Confucius, who had called on T. S. Eliot in London and been the Paris editor of the *Paris Review*, for which he had interviewed Robert Lowell. If he wasn't royalty, he had at least touched it. On the telephone he always said, *Phil, my boy, how are you?* in the most sophisticated voice I'd ever heard, very precise, as if his concourse were typically with the gods but he'd learned English as a second language so he could order lunch. He had what was called a Harvard accent, but it sounded like money to me. He never failed to ask what I thought of his latest poem, continued asking long after I'd given him sufficient reason to stop. What could I tell him? I was on deadline every time we spoke, with headlines and photo captions still to write, and stories to cut to make them fit on the page. I didn't read his poems with the care they deserved until the next morning, before the hum of the day began, when I could sit with a cup of coffee in my hand and my feet up on my desk, the paper spread in my lap. They were by far the most interesting thing on offer, perhaps the most interesting writing to appear in those pages since Charles Dow and Edward Jones had changed the name of their daily news bulletin for Wall Street traders, the *Customers' Afternoon Letter,* in 1889. Dude, I wanted to tell him, I can't believe you're getting away with this in the *Wall Street Journal!* You're my hero! But I didn't want to be fawning, so I'd focus on a particular stanza whose music I liked, or a particular image that struck me, avoiding mention of the lines I caressed most dearly: *Put the pills back in the vial. / Put the gun back in the drawer. / Ventilate the carbon monoxide. / Back away from the railing.* I think he believed that I wasn't a very bright boy, a fact I confirmed when one time he asked me what else would be appearing on the next morning's page, alongside his poem. I mentioned a piece on the Elgin Marbles, and he took a quick, shallow breath, aghast. *EL-jin, my boy,* he said in that godlike voice of his. *EL-jin!* Never having heard the word spoken aloud, I'd pronounced the *g* as you would in god, which to a certain cast of mind was akin to calling Socrates *sock-RAT-us.*

Around this time there began to be heard complaints about the political thrust and aesthetic sensibilities of the Lei-sure & Arts page. Ray mentioned these complaints to me in elliptical asides during conversations on other matters. He'd apparently been forwarded some scolding letters to the editor about a couple of Seidel's poems; he'd also received a memo from the publisher that raised concerns about propriety and sound judgment. But Ray was a cagey fellow, a survivor of twenty years in the shadow of Bob Bartley, and although I never asked him how he responded to questions about his stewardship, I imagined him pointing out that the occasional kerfuffle proved he had his readers' attention, and besides, every single day a big fat ad appeared on his page.

We were, after all, in the midst of a millennial madness, and the paper was not just an avid chronicler of the madness but an active participant in it. One month after I was origi-nally hired, the Dow Jones Industrial Average—comprised of thirty corporations chosen by the managing editor of the *Wall Street Journal,* and the only company brand more rec-ognizable than the paper itself—closed above 10,000 for the first time. The *Journal* celebrated this triumph with a banner six-column headline, only the third in its history, the others having blared the news of the bombing of Pearl Harbor and the start of the First Gulf War.

On March 10, 2000, the NASDAQ index reached an all-time high of 5,048.62. The paper was so fat with tech-company advertising, the average subscriber—white, fiftyish, male, with a yearly household income of around $200,000—risked a herniated disk when he lifted it from his doorstep. Management went on a hiring spree to fill an ever greater need for copy, and the paper hatched new daily sections and weekly supplements to cash in on the advertising lucre of companies that would go belly up before the end of their second fiscal year. I knew colleagues who charged every movie, every dinner out, every new book or bottle of high-end wine to their Dow Jones credit cards. Ad managers at the paper's sister publication, *Barron's*, were said to keep open tabs at various Manhattan bars and entertain clients by expensing the cost of strippers.

It was easy to be carried along on this tide of giddy prosperity, writing the occasional, mildly subversive piece in order to cling to what I thought of as possession of my soul. The paper promised an audience of millions, and a part of me couldn't quite shake the idea that the goal of writing was to have your work read by as many people as possible. Once a month or so I'd propose an article for the Leisure & Arts page, and more often than not Ray would go for it. By almost any yardstick I'd lucked out in my professional life. I could have lived in Bismarck, or Dubuque, like some of my old college friends, writing stories about city council meetings. I could have been waiting tables in a Lower East Side tapas bar. Instead I saw jazz for free in any club I cared to visit, just by calling ahead and telling the doorman where I worked. When out-of-towners came to visit, I took them to Windows on the World, just across the street from the office, a view that never failed to awe. If I profiled a writer or musician—Larry McMurtry, Charlie Haden—the subject's latest book or album shot up the Amazon sales rankings. I was, for a moment anyway, moving units and meeting people.

I built a sweet home library from the spoils of the weekly book giveaway, the constant pile of review copies sent by American publishers to the paper's literary editor. Not only did I make off with reissued classics from Penguin and the Modern Library, I surreptitiously swiped the volumes on tantric sex, slipping them into my bag when no one else was looking. When uttered during the exchange of small talk at parties in Brooklyn tenements—always somewhat sheepishly, and only in response to direct questions about my gainful employment—the words *Wall Street Journal* had the effect of a potent narcotic: dilated pupils, flushed face, and what I perceived as a perceptible slackening of sexual inhibition, of which, being a socially awkward midwesterner, I rarely had the courage to take advantage, despite my collection of books on tantric sex.

My new apartment was a one-bedroom, second-story walkup in Queens, on the border of Astoria and Long Island City, four stops to Manhattan on the N train. It had been trashed pretty badly by the previous occupants, the only reason it wasn't gone before I came across the listing. When the landlord showed me the place he apologized for its condition, but I was desperate. I offered him a deal. I'd repaint the whole thing floor to ceiling, lay new tile in the kitchen, tear up the worn purple carpet in the living room, and sand and refinish the wood floors—if he'd waive the security deposit and give me the first three months rent-free. He looked at me as if I were insane, but I'd done the math—I'd save more than two grand—and when I extended my hand, he shook it.

I removed the carpet only to discover little drifts of mouse turds along the walls, plus cockroach corpses by the dozen. The new paint job required multiple coats to cover the underlying shade of Pepto-Bismol pink. I rented a large circular sander for the wood floors and applied sealer every other day in strips so I could move from room to room without ruining the finish. The work took almost every spare waking minute I had over three weeks, and the smells of paint and polyurethane were a long time in fading. Still, it was satisfying to live alone again—no roommate, no feral cats—and in a neighborhood where I had no trouble blending in: middle class, ethnically diverse, with a Mediterranean flavor thanks to the one of the largest expat populations of Greeks in the world.

Though I finally had a set of rooms all my own, I found my new freedom slightly unnerving. Unlike in Bed-Stuy, there were plenty of restaurants and bars and cafés within a short walk of my apartment. The options for whiling away an evening overwhelmed me with their variety; I couldn't seem to find the place to call mine, the place where a loner could sit cocooned in silence and remain unremarked-upon, unseen.

Committing to the life of a loner involves one difficulty above all others: even loners, perhaps especially loners, often find themselves horny. In New York whole industries thrived on the basis of this simple fact, and nowhere was this more evident than in the *Village Voice* classifieds. I began to study those pages with what I thought of as a detached and almost scholarly amusement, but one ad in particular kept calling to me with the promise of amateur phone sex. The very existence of amateur phone sex intrigued me. I'd always assumed it was a realm for professionals.

It wasn't long before I memorized the prerecorded greeting. I even learned to mimic the perky-bimbo inflections of the woman who recited it:

Thanks for calling the all-live, all-the-time phone line where ladies call free to share their fantasies with you. If you're under eighteen, you must hang up. . . .

Welcome to the exciting new way to talk one-on-one with the area's hottest students, housewives, and working girls for just thirty-five cents per minute, seventy-five for the first. . . .

I knew the city's hottest students, housewives, and working girls weren't sitting at home pressing speed-dial with one hand while petting themselves with the other, but when I called that first night I thought I might get lucky and connect with an introverted bombshell, a naughty librarian. We'd talk about music or books or the Kyoto Protocol. We'd choose a place to meet for a drink. We'd proceed to her place, or mine, and lick each other's privates in the dark.

Half the single people my age in New York were already using the Internet as a portal to erotic adventure, but I'd always been a little slow adopting new technologies. It was the new millennium and I was still using a manual typewriter.

Main menu: Press one for sexy recorded personals, or press two for live connections on the talk line.

I pressed two.

Press one to talk to women, or press two to talk to men.

I pressed one.

Live talk main menu: Press one to connect with callers who are on the line right now. Press two to record or update your dateline personals greeting.

I pressed one.

You have ninety seconds to describe who you are and what you're interested in. Take care with your privacy— no full names, addresses, or other information that could be abused by other callers. Here's your chance to make an introduction. The most intriguing greetings get the most responses, so make your ad as sexy as you can. Your privacy is guaranteed. Your greeting will play only to others who are on the talk line when you are. To remove your greeting, just hang up. You can rerecord as often as you need to, until you're satisfied. Start speaking at the tone. Press pound when you're done. Good luck.

I was drearily earnest at first. I stressed my status as a

gainfully employed, suit-wearing monkey. I laid on the midwestern charm, the whole small-town-boy-in-the-big-city act. I waxed poetic about my love of music and books, going to museums, eating out. I was, in short, Prince Charming, a perfect gentleman straight from the script of a rom-com, just the push of a button away.

Welcome to the talk line!

Rarely have I heard such scorn. Women sent recorded messages in which they simply cackled at me. Some were incredulous: *You're actually looking for a date? On this line?* One even presumed to judge my anatomy: *Come on, little boy, pull that itsy-bitsy, teeny-weenie out of your pants and play with momma. . . .*

I hung up that first night completely demoralized. I wanted to be appalled at all the perverts and misfits on their telephones across the city—the heavy-breathers, the pre-op transsexuals, the women from the Bronx looking to play for pay—but I was mostly disappointed in myself. They, at least, were candid about what they wanted.

And what did I want? There's no way I could have been honest about that. What was I supposed to say: I need someone to sleep with me so I can tell the story of my brother's death? That would have had the virtue of being true, as if the truth were a virtue on a phone-sex line. Over the course of a few short-lived flings in the time since Dan's suicide, I'd discovered that sex emptied my mind of everything nonessential, and the one thing that remained essential, I thought, was the story of his suicide. Everything else was a dream or an anecdote. Nothing else meant a thing, not compared with the big story, and I just couldn't talk about it unless I'd bared myself in physical intimacy. Hard to imagine working that up as an attractive come-on, though: *Hey, sweetheart, let's screw with our eyes closed and then snuggle up for some pillow talk about the mysteries of self-inflicted death. Will you listen if I tell you?*

In time I worked through my initial misgivings about phone sex. I did the practical thing. I listened and learned. The rules were simple. You could lie about what you looked like—who would know the difference?—but you'd best be blunt about your desires if you didn't want to waste anyone's time. It was all there for the ear, an aural smorgasbord of titillation and perversion, thirty-five cents per minute, seventy-five for the first, every kinky fantasy you've ever heard about and more, and plenty of people willing to pay and be paid for real-world sex. You listened, one after another, to little personal ads ("greetings") in the voice of the person being personal, and make no mistake, they were personal, about everything under the sun from golden showers to gang bangs, with an emphasis on interracial pleasure seeking and an unmistakable undertone of pitiful desperation.

Press one to repeat this greeting. Press two to send a private message. Press three to ask this caller to connect with you live, one-on-one. Press four to hear the next caller's greeting. Press five to return to the previous ad. Press seven to block this caller from contacting you.

With a bit of practice I developed a whole portfolio of

personae, ranging from the iconic to the cryptic. Clark Kent Calling from a Phone Booth was my go-to line. His ready-made image allowed me to dispense with laborious physical description. He was also the perfect fantasy man of the women's magazines—a reliable breadwinner, a modest but hunky journalist who morphed into Superman when he took off his clothes.

Super-Exhibitionistic Horse-Cock Boy was a bit of inspired ad-lib. One night I made up a story about masturbating in front of my living room window while a neighbor woman watched me from her kitchen across the courtyard. Messages flooded in. Everyone wanted to hear about it. Part of the allure of an amateur sex line involved its invitation to be playful with the rituals of the form: it felt appropriate to situate the fantasy itself inside an act of voyeurism.

The Sound of One Hand Slapping was a late addition to my repertoire, and by no means original; I heard many masterly variations. I merely put my own spin on an old phone-sex standard. The trick, of course, was in the execution. I tried at first for authenticity, recording an actual masturbatory stroke, but it was too subtle for the mouthpiece to pick up, and I kept getting a prerecorded admonition: *I'm sorry, your message must be at least ten seconds long. Please try again.* At first I misheard this as: *I'm sorry, your member must be at least ten inches long. Please try again.* I experimented until I found a plausible substitute, which involved rubbing my index finger back and forth across the mouthpiece. When I replayed the message to confirm it, I heard a sound that hinted at some sort of deviant friction. By pressing my fingertip with greater or lesser force, I could create a stylized rendition of vigorous, almost violent copulation, or gentle, sensuous cock-stroking. (Later I even recorded an actual slap, although I struck my thigh instead of my ass, having learned that on the talk line impression *is* reality.) The virtue of this method arose from its ambiguity, its invitation for others to initiate the fantasy. It allowed me, in the opening joust of a phone fuck, to shield my voice from other callers.

I'd dialed so often my voice had become a known quantity.

Once I got hooked I had to make a real effort not to call every night. Evenings when I stayed away from the phone tended to play out in the same way. I'd be abducted by one of my blue moods, a combination of loneliness and claustrophobia at the thought of all the human longing playing out in the towers and the streets, in the privacy of little urban rooms. I'd run out of patience for reading, my usual strategy of escape, so I'd pace my apartment, listening to Lester Young and Coleman Hawkins, until I tired of retracing my steps. I'd take my notebook and go for a beer at one of the Irish joints in my neighborhood: O'Hanlon's, McCann's, McCaffrey & Burke. There was always something soothing in the murmur of voices and the clank of glassware, men and sometimes even a few women talking in the smoky, intimate light. I liked to imagine I'd find a beautiful woman sipping whiskey all alone in the corner. Our eyes would meet. I'd buy her a drink. We'd step, just for a moment, from the frame of the Hopper painting that circumscribed our lives.

Or maybe we'd step *into* the frame, create a moment of melancholy beauty we could hold with us forever.

No matter. She was never there.

One night my friend Rachel called me at home. It was rare to hear her voice but always a pleasure when it happened. We'd met during our respective internships at the *Nation* and the *Village Voice* and had kept in touch, mostly by letter, me from Montana, her from Seattle, then later me from New York and her from Virginia.

Toward the end of our brief season in the city I'd confessed my attraction to her, a confession she did not reciprocate, though I sensed no worse than ambivalence in her cryptic silence. Problem was, she had a boyfriend. But now her boyfriend had gone abroad, to study international relations at the London School of Economics, while she pursued a master's in poetry at the University of Virginia. I'd met the boyfriend once. He was a very small fellow with unwashed hair, tiny round glasses, and tremendous, outsized hands. You couldn't not notice his beautiful hands.

Rachel told me those hands had found another woman to reach for in her absence. He'd called and confessed this to her, two months after the fact. She told him it was over. He immediately flew to Virginia in an act of contrition. They wept, they cursed; they held each other tenderly, they screwed not very tenderly. Then he left for London. Nothing was resolved. She was alone with her wounds, alone in Charlottesville, Virginia. He called again and again and pleaded with her to give him another chance. He swore he'd prove his devotion, if only she would grant him one more chance.

She could not do that. Instead she called me.

She said she'd never stopped thinking about what it would be like to be involved with me. I hadn't known she'd ever started—and besides, I wanted to say now, it would probably be a nightmare to be involved with me. But I stayed mum.

She said she'd been adept at disguising her attraction, but it had been there all along.

Adept is too pale a word, I told her.

She wanted to come out and say something but didn't know if it was appropriate. She admitted she felt oddly giddy and drunk, as if she were capable, suddenly, of anything, and this scared her, made her think that she should play things close to the vest.

Go ahead, I said. Say it anyway. What's to lose?

Our friendship, she said.

We'll always be friends, I said.

Almost as if changing the subject, she said she'd be spending spring break in upstate New York, at her father's country home. But she wasn't changing the subject.

What train would I take to get there? I asked.

She told me the line and the station stop, said she'd happily meet me on arrival.

Nine days later I was there.

The country home was sprawling and drafty, nearly three hundred years old, with low ceilings and a thriving resident population of mice. Her father, a theater producer, made it clear that he was not to be bothered unless we had ideas about where he could find the money to stage an adaptation of one of Thomas Mann's lesser novels. He gave me the once-over and then dialed someone on the phone.

After a tour of the grounds, Rachel and I walked down a long dirt road and sat in a field of what had been alfalfa the year before. The sun was warm on our faces, and we reclined at the crest of a hill where we could see out over a valley to the low mountains that rose on the far side. As the sun dropped behind her it turned her auburn hair a fiery gold. I wanted badly to kiss her but lacked the courage to move near enough to her mouth.

We walked down the hill amid the springtime smells of melting water and pine needles. I knew I would remember that afternoon with perfect clarity for the rest of my life—the blue sky, the geese and their honking overhead, the light on her hair and her nervous half-smile, the smell of dust off the road. The anticipation of how sweet and soft her lips would be.

After dinner that night she handed me a letter she'd written a couple of days earlier. She said she'd wanted to write one last time before everything changed. Then she left the room, and I sat in the lamplight, reading.

The letter closed by saying, *This is a goodbye kiss to everything that has come before.* It was a beautiful piece of writing, funny and sweet and passionate; it even included a long meditation on the beauty and eroticism of the word *passion*. I didn't quite know what to think about what was happening between us. I'd always wanted to be more than friends. She'd always insisted we couldn't be more than friends. I'd finally made my peace with that, and now the tables had turned. She was the one in pursuit, after I'd given up. I was more nervous now than when my feelings had gone unreciprocated. I'd become quite comfortable with my feelings going unreciprocated. Preemptive rejection kept the stakes manageable.

I sat alone with her letter for a long time. When she returned she held a glass of red wine for each of us.

I'm sick of boys, do you know that? she said. All I've ever had are boys. It's time I had an adult relationship.

We drank the wine. We went upstairs together. It felt like an adult situation. We undressed and went to the bed. I was feeling more adult by the moment. After some exploratory caressing, we agreed that we'd be wiser to stop before we went too far, wait for another time when we'd be more comfortable, more sure in each other's presence—our adult selves asserting some objective analysis on potential outcomes.

I told her I had all the patience in the world.

Coming from any other guy, she said, I wouldn't believe that for a moment. But from you I do.

As if to disabuse her of her foolishness, I began to kiss her stomach, her thighs. It wasn't long before we were doing exactly what we had said we weren't going to do.

As we lay tangled in the sheets, she said, I had no idea you were so religious.

What do you mean?

You kept saying, Oh my god, oh my god.

I guess I must have. But doesn't everyone?

I thought Catholic school had taken all of that out of you.

No, I said, I've merely found a new altar at which to worship.

We raked the yard in the late morning sun, exposing the fecund smell of wet, decaying leaves, the wetness trapped since autumn. She exuded elegance even in yard work, elegance in posture, an elegant wool sweater just so on her shoulders, that shy half-smile she smiled to herself that signified her mind at play. I'd never known a woman more attractive in the act of thinking. I saw in my own mind her naked body, its dips and arcing lines, petite navel, small nipples on ample breasts, powerful yet graceful thighs and calves. Cheeks round and red as plums. A delicate, slender neck. Biceps firm from regular games of squash. Pale skin and eyes of a glacial blue, a sprinkle of freckles on her face. We walked through the woods along a little creek. She tried to leap across the water and landed in mud. Her shoe, covered in slime, made a sucking sound when she pulled it free. We laughed and laughed.

In an open swath of grass the sun-bleached bones of an animal, the size of a small dog, lay in the very shape in which it must have died—except the skull, which was a foot away and facing back upon the rest of itself, in terror or bemusement it was hard to tell. We noted this and moved on, a tiny fissure in the texture of the day.

In bed that night she said, I don't want to lose control. Not yet. If I let you get me off, everything will change.

Hasn't it changed already?

I mean really change.

She said every decision she'd made in the previous three years was now called into question. She doubted that anything she'd done was due to passion. With her boyfriend she'd found comfort, someone who wouldn't challenge her, who provided stability and familiarity—the safe and reliable college beau. So much for stability, reliability. She'd gone with him to Seattle after college to escape the hard choices of life out of school, when suddenly all of one's options are narrowed, when you finally have to figure out who to be. She'd wanted a sabbatical from decision making. She'd wanted a sojourn of sea-smelling air and Asian-Pacific cuisine, a lush landscape of emerald-green. Now something inside of her was ignited, and she wanted more. Her mind was on fire and her body with it. Her head crackled with ideas. She wanted to write for real. She wanted to create again. Her master's program in Virginia challenged her to think more deeply. Her boyfriend's departure and betrayal liberated her to feel more intensely.

So this is what it feels like to make love to a liberated woman, I said.

I'll show you a liberated woman, she said.

After she'd shown me, I told her that every decision I'd made in the past three years could be traced to the death of my brother. I recounted how one of my uncles had mentioned that I was the likelier candidate for a self-inflicted death; I admitted that although his death had been unbearably sad in the beginning I'd found a way to take a kind of grim pleasure in it. It was the black heart of my life; it gave my life a bleak grandeur it would have lacked otherwise. I'd come to treasure that grandeur. Careless bliss and unspoiled contentment were for the simpleminded.

He had revealed the secret passageway off to the side of the life we all led. He'd pulled the curtain on the central fact of existence, which until then I'd failed to comprehend as more than an abstraction: life was optional. From the far end of that passageway he beckoned, mutely suggestive, wrapped in mystery. This was the unmentionable secret at the center of my days in the time since his death: the fact that he was always with me, though dimly remembered and void of substance, like a phantom limb.

So this is what it feels like to have a threesome, she said.

I've never known anyone to make a joke about my brother, I said.

I'm not trying to be callous, but don't you think it's past time?

Maybe.

And about what your uncle said—

Not tonight. Let it go.

Exactly, she said. Let it go.

I soon became familiar with the long train ride to Charlottesville, the halting, slowly accelerating departure, newspapers and books shielding faces, drinks in the jolly bar car.

Strange intimacies with strangers, the proffered stories and the swiveled glances. The endless telephone poles and the scalloped pattern of their lines, rising and falling, rising and falling out the windows. The filthy ditches and the piles of gravel and the scrap-metal heaps. Long lengths of gleaming metal pipes stacked in pyramid form. Featureless glass office towers, low-slung factories abandoned to rot. Brick bungalows and back yard swings. The huge neon sign on the Delaware River Bridge, part boast, part lament: TRENTON MAKES—THE WORLD TAKES.

She must have known that my devotion to our correspondence hinted at larger devotions; yet I wondered how something so powerful could have remained dormant all this time, or if not dormant then at least hidden. She was a mysterious creature, sensuous in the way she moved, self-possessed in the extreme, yet beneath the calm exterior a fierce intelligence burned, a hunger for ideas and language. When I arrived at her apartment the first time, she insisted on reading aloud to me the last eight pages of Don DeLillo's first novel, *Americana*, which she'd just finished. Then she ordered me to carry her to the bed. We spent the rest of the afternoon there in the warm yellow light, delicious hours of indulgent pleasure.

How sweet the taste of stolen bread.

The next day, while we made dinner, the phone rang. By the way her face changed when she answered it, I knew it was her boyfriend. He told her he'd received her letter, in which she'd flatly stated their relationship was over. He couldn't let himself believe it. There must be someone else, he said. She did not answer. In that silence there's a name, he said. There is someone, isn't there?

She hung up the phone.

Later, while we were lying next to each other in the dark, she said, It scares me to say this. But I know as long as I live I'm never going to feel about anyone the way I feel about you. I'm never going to find someone who makes me feel so good about myself. I respect you. I respect your need for freedom.

That's the beauty of this, I said. We respect the other person's needs. I don't think we come to this with blinders on. We can have freedom in togetherness.

Guardians of each other's solitude, she said.

Yes. Guardians of each other's solitude.

We appeared to agree on everything that mattered. We could have each other. We could have our work. We could have our space in which to think and create and we could do it in nearness to a lover.

I allowed myself to believe we could have it all.

At the end of her spring semester she came to New York for nine days. We went out most nights, drank martinis and smoked expensive cigarettes, ate Vietnamese food in Chinatown, walked through SoHo and the West Village, hopping from bar to bar. She tried to educate me on the poetry criticism she'd been reading, Randall Jarrell and Helen Vendler. I tried to interest her in the novels I'd been reading, *The Virgin Suicides* and *The Pure and the Impure*. We confessed our dreams of writing something great, professed our desire to support each other in the work of doing so.

You have an idealized vision of me, she said one night. I can't possibly live up to it. I think you'll be disappointed eventually. I'm afraid of that.

I wanted to assure her it wouldn't happen; if anything, I'd disappoint her. Of course she wasn't some angel. She wasn't perfect. But all I knew of her, all I could intuit, intrigued me. Even her moodiness when hungry charmed me. Rather than be wounded by her testy tongue, I was moved to feed her. I wanted to learn the art of taking care, and anyway she mostly took care of herself, and happily. She avoided making me a perpetual human-improvement project. I did her the same courtesy. We each had our flaws—mine were impossible to hide—but we had no urge to modify them in each other. I began with an image of her and wanted only to add understanding and nuance and roll with the punches. I didn't want her to conform to my image. I wanted her to expand and complicate it. Or so I told myself.

She did so in spades one night when I made some stray comment concerning my notebooks. They were my repository of toxic thoughts and unspeakable dreams, my testing ground for scenes and ideas, my suicide commonplace book, my sanctuary of the mind. Mention of them cast a shadow over her face. It was there suddenly, and just as suddenly it was gone, and I knew the passing shadow meant that she had read them. I said, You didn't, did you? She twisted her face in shame and said yes. She admitted she'd gone looking for herself, gone looking for my most candid thoughts about her. It was narcissistic, she said. I wanted to know what you had written about me. It was that simple.

Only a few days earlier I had told her it would be over if she ever dared violate my private writings. I'll throw you out on your ass, I said. That will be it. *Finito.* Done. My trust would be destroyed.

We were no longer in the realm of the hypothetical. My threat had backfired. Instead of warning her off, I'd fueled her curiosity, made her think there were things worth reading in those mad scribblings.

For everything else she was, aside from a narcissistic snoop—witty, well read, a great beauty, a kind soul, a sporting lover—I decided I should try to forgive her.

So you want to know my secrets? I said.

Is this a trap? she said.

I'll tell you my secrets. You don't need to go hunting for them.

I don't know if I want to hear this.

You can handle it.

You think?

I do. Here's one: I fear I'll one day put a gun to my head, to know what that feels like, to bring myself closer to the one person I can't seem to reach another way.

Um, okay.

Also, I could have saved him. That's the big one. I had my chance. I could have saved him but I betrayed him with selfishness and inattention.

I don't buy it.

I knew you wouldn't. I don't expect you to. But it's true.

She sat for a long time in silence.

Do you really believe that? she said at last.

I've thought about it almost every day since he died, I said.

Here's what I think, she said. I think what *he* did was the ultimate act of selfishness. And you're one of the casualties. You didn't kill him. He killed himself. But you can't bring yourself to blame him, so you've got to go looking for suspects, and the most convenient one to finger is yourself.

A fury rose within me, an urge to defend him, but I couldn't think of how, so I held my tongue.

Be clear what it is you're mourning, she said. You're not mourning what you had. You're mourning what can never be. You're mourning the loss of possibilities.

I wanted to tell her she was wrong, or maybe just glib. I wanted to tell her that the manner of the death made a difference in the manner of the mourning. I wanted to tell her that a suicide bequeathed the grieving a unique blend of emotions—anger and guilt first among them—and an intensity of regret otherwise unknown in the human experience. But I feared her superior education, her wider breadth of reference. She'd probably run circles around me, leaving me feeling lousy about how poorly I understood the central event of my life, and I didn't need it, not that night—I was too invested in my own mythology; I'd exposed myself and been told I was wrong—so I rolled over and pretended to sleep.

We honed a routine of twice-weekly telephone talks, occasional visits to the other's city, afternoons in bed whenever possible, followed by nights on the town. We tinkered with the definition of our situation. For a time we were having an affair. For a time we were boyfriend-girlfriend. For a time we were even something like friends with benefits, free to see other people. Depending on the week, we were either in cahoots or in love, or all of the above.

Bob Bartley and I talked so infrequently I remember every occasion with uncanny clarity. I even recorded these encounters in my journal, they were so strange and suggestive. The first time, he asked if I would proofread something he'd written. I didn't want to proofread his work, but you don't say no to the most important person at the world's most important publication.

I read the column. I disagreed with everything in it, but it was powerfully written. That was the unmistakable thing about his editorials—even if you thought they were crude ideological screeds, as they almost invariably were, they left you with no doubt about what he believed. He claimed to craft everything he wrote for optimum "muzzle velocity," as he once put it to another journalist. His style owed a great deal to the old yellow journalism of personal invective; he didn't just savage his opponents' ideas, he aimed to obliterate his opponents altogether, or at least ream them with a rusty poker for their intellectual bankruptcy, their moral cretinism.

I told him I saw only one mistake. He'd made the words "pipe dream" one word, with no space between them. I told him it should be two words, according to *Webster's New World Dictionary*, which was my authoritative source in such matters.

He told me he didn't care what *Webster's New World Dictionary* said. It was his editorial, and he wanted pipe dream to be one word: *pipedream*. He said I should delete the space I'd inserted between pipe and dream.

I did.

We talked a second time a few months later. I was standing in the hallway with a colleague from the Leisure & Arts page, and Bob Bartley approached us. He said he had two doctors' appointments on the Upper East Side of Manhattan the next day. He had a bit of leisure time to spare between them, and wondered if there was any art worth seeing at the museums on the Upper East Side.

I said, Yes, there's a wonderful show of Walker Evans photos at the Met.

He said, Thanks, I may have a look at that.

A few days later I met him in the hallway. I said hello.

He did not say hello.

I said, Bob, did you see the Walker Evans show at the Met?

He stopped and looked at me. I wondered if I should have called him Mr. Bartley.

He said, Yes, I saw it.

What did you think?

It wasn't for me, he said. I stayed for five minutes and went to the Egyptian galleries.

Walker Evans was, among other things, a great documentarian of Depression-era southern poverty; Bob Bartley was appalled by the very idea of poor people. He'd once told the *Washington Post Magazine* that he didn't think there were any poor people left in America, "just a few hermits or something like that." To Bob Bartley, Walker Evans's photos were a form of pornography that depicted human beings in a sinful state of filth and depravity, and such images had no place in an American museum.

Of course I disagreed. Not only did I appreciate the unadorned honesty of Walker Evans's photographs, I'd grown up in a poor family myself. As a child coming of age on a farm where we couldn't make enough money to get by, I'd stood in line with my mother at the community hall in Currie, Minnesota, for handouts of surplus government cheese. Pictures of people like us from the time of the Great Depression hung in many museums, farmers too broke to feed themselves without government help.

Bob Bartley didn't believe the government should be in the cheese-handout business.

Rachel came to visit during her winter break. She was working on a long paper and wanted someplace quiet to hole up and write. My apartment served nicely, as I was gone each day for ten hours. I'd come home from work to find her in bed, exactly where I'd left her, surrounded by a scattering of papers. Wound up from copyediting against deadline, I'd pour myself a glass of bourbon and put some Miles Davis on the stereo, cook us dinner. The music didn't bother her. She stayed in the bedroom, naked, unshowered, writing intently. I made it my duty to see that she ate, since she claimed to be uninterested in food, only words, ideas. I brought her cold drinks. When she panicked at the prospect of running out of paper, I went to the stationery store and bought a stack of legal pads. I was doing my best to be the handmaiden to creativity. That's what I would have wanted from her.

I took her at her word that she was on to something, a new theory, a work of genius. I could hardly tell her to stop; that would have been heresy to both of us. If you're working and it's flowing, you run with it. The muse didn't visit very often, so you had to give yourself over like a love slave when she did.

I assumed at first that her claims to genius were at least tinged with irony. On the third evening she began to frighten me. She'd hardly slept. She talked in great strings of sentences, making metaphors one after another. I sat on the edge of the bed and listened as her pronouncements became ever more grandiose. She claimed she was channeling James Joyce. She said she was rewriting the Book of Genesis. She was drawing a map for the politics of a new era. She was going to touch off a peaceful revolution, achieve what Marx had only dreamed of.

She was going mad in my bedroom.

It's the year one, she said. It's a politics for an age of information overload. The only difference between words and worlds is a typographical error. The only difference between immodality and immorality is a typographical error. I'm writing a bible for our times. It's going to change everything. George Bush won't bring peace to the Middle East. I will. I'm going to show the way. I'm going to have enemies, and they're going to want to put me away in an institution. I'm going to tell them I'm already in an institution. The University of Virginia is my institution. I'm going to make geniuses of everyone in the world. I'm going to succeed where Jesus failed.

How? I asked.

Because Jesus was not a woman. Because women weren't allowed to paint and act and study philosophy and math and they weren't allowed to write. I'm the first. I'm the female Jesus.

I told her that she was scaring me, that she sounded delusional, but she only laughed at me with pity.

You'll see, she said. Maybe you should just go away for a while. Come back when I'm finished. Then you can read it and know.

I left to run some errands. I stayed away for hours, stopped in a bar for drinks, hoping that by the time I returned she'd have left.

She hadn't moved.

She started calling herself a mystic and a prophet. She claimed that if only she could sit down with Hillary Clinton, one-on-one, and teach her to see the world through the theory of the oneness of everything, then Mrs. Clinton would become our next President and the world would never again experience want or war. I began to argue with her, my voice rising in frustration. She remained unperturbed. She said she was sad that I couldn't see the future the way she could, but that one day soon I would. I would see and I would understand. She would help me along to the place where she was, and there we'd be partners in bliss.

The next morning she stuffed her papers in a bag and left for the train to her father's place. Some of her clothes remained scattered in the bedroom. She didn't say a proper goodbye, just walked out the door in mismatched socks, her unwashed hair twisted in little pretzel shapes. I loathed myself for the relief I felt once she was gone. I was scared she might never be the same, that by encouraging her, replenishing her paper supply and bringing her dinner in bed, telling her all the while to keep writing, I'd unwittingly chauffeured the vehicle that had driven her over the edge.

I called Rachel's father, but he didn't answer. I left a message telling him to be alert for changes in his daughter's state of mind. Then I caught the train to work and tried not to think about any of it. But when I got back home I looked up some half-remembered lines of Seidel:

> You said you were Baudelaire—
> Or was it Marlowe?—
> You said you were Blake
> Talking English with the angels,
> And said you were Christ, of course,
> But *never* would say
> You were yourself.

They appeared in a poem called "Hart Crane Near the End," and I didn't need reminding how he'd met his.

Her father saw right away that something was wrong. It took forty-eight hours to get Rachel an appointment to see her longtime therapist. After talking to Rachel for fifteen minutes, the shrink advised admitting her to a psychiatric emergency room, ASAP. The shrink's secretary called an ambulance. The cops arrived. They spoke to the shrink, who told them what the situation was: a manic episode gone out of control. The cops then talked to Rachel, who calmly convinced them she was fine. An argument ensued among Rachel's father, the therapist, and the cops. While they argued, Rachel slipped away and vanished into the city, but before she left she told another therapist that if she were forced to go to the hospital she'd kill herself. She did not want to be held captive. She would not stand for it.

Rachel's father called me at work, told me Rachel was on the lam. If I saw her or heard from her I was to call immediately. I hurried through my work of fitting headlines, writing photo captions, proofing copy, then I rushed for the elevator, hustled over West Street on the pedestrian bridge, and crossed Liberty Street to the subway station beneath the World Trade Center towers. I took an uptown N to Fourteenth Street, caught the East Side express to Fifty-ninth, transferred back to the N train home. No message on the machine; no sign she'd been in the apartment.

I ate a bowl of soup. I paced. I called two of her friends in New York but neither one answered.

There was a knock at the door, firmer than she would have knocked. I squinted through the peephole at two cops. I opened the door. They flashed their badges, offered their names. They asked if I'd seen her recently. I told them it had been a couple of days.

Do you mind if we come in? one of them asked.

Not at all.

Just a formality, the other said. Gotta make sure she's not cut up in pieces in your tub.

They sauntered around the apartment, thumbs hooked in their belts, leaning torso-first through doorways. I heard the curtain rings slide back and forth on the shower rod.

The cops thanked me and left.

An hour later she rang the buzzer, three large shopping bags in her arms, a new pair of shoes on her feet. She told me she'd eaten a nice dinner and had her nails done. Afterward, she went inside a Catholic church somewhere in Manhattan, sat in the back pew.

I heard breathing, she said. And whispering. Like the devil was whispering in my ear. I could tell because the voice spoke with a forked tongue.

She went on about rectifying Einstein's inadvertent creation of the atom bomb, using her vision to reveal the secrets of the unity of matter encoded in the invisible digits of zeros and ones that undergirded the vast computer web. She said she'd discovered a theory that would have saved Virginia

Woolf and Sylvia Plath from suicide, if only she'd been able to share it with them.

When she went to the bathroom, I called her father.

Just stay with her tonight, her father said. I'll come get her in the morning.

Rachel emerged from the bathroom and gave me a funny look. I tried to stay calm as a fury of helplessness rose inside of me.

I'm sorry, I said, what's the plan again?

Silence on the other end.

I think sooner is better, I said.

Okay. I'll call the cops and have them come right over.

Fifteen minutes later, the same two cops came to the door. The look on Rachel's face when she saw them absolutely crushed me.

You didn't, she said. You didn't just betray me.

I'm sorry. It's for the better.

You backstabbing son of a bitch, she said. You dirty Judas!

I rode with her in the ambulance, held her hand. For the first time she looked scared. She said she'd known all along that her genius would be punished, she just hadn't expected me to be among her punishers.

Her father met us at the hospital. He explained the situation to the intake nurse. Two other nurses coaxed Rachel onto a gurney and wheeled her down a dismal hallway, through a set of doors. We heard a shriek, then a long, piercing wail.

We later learned they'd strapped her down and injected her with Haldol and Benadryl, a typical welcome-to-the-psych-ward cocktail.

The next time I saw her was in a private room at Mount Sinai Medical Center, a few days later. She was heavily doped on a combination of drugs whose names I couldn't keep straight. She still professed visions, warned against the unseen and disruptive powers of static electricity. I didn't know who she was anymore, or what she was in the process of becoming. I feared she might never come back, which made me scared for her, and almost as scared for me. Her psychotic break confirmed a thing I'd long suspected, that if I let people get too close to me they were doomed; she later admitted that in the worst of her mania she'd been gripped by visions of my brother as described in the journals of mine she'd read, those grotesque gropings toward understanding him by imagining his brain sprayed on the wall.

They brought a man in, she said. A big black man, and they did the same thing to him that they did to me. They held him down on the bed and put a needle in his arm, and he screamed just like I did, and I said, Don't you see? He's human and he needs to be touched with love and not poked by your instruments. They told me to go away and shut up. It's not your concern. Go away. It's not your concern. They said it over and over.

She turned and spoke to her nurse.

You're a healer. I like how you treat me. You don't poke me with anything. You touch me. You hold my hand. You're helping me come back to the ground. It got scary up there.

I began to visit her every day. Sometimes she was happy to see me. Other times she hardly appeared to notice I was there. She'd long since stopped asking questions of anyone. She slept, or watched TV, or read and reread the get-well cards she'd been sent.

It's so beautiful, she said. So beautiful. Everyone is together. My mom is laughing with me. She brought me chocolates and flowers and lots of gifts. She never did that before. This is what I want, exactly what I want. I'm so happy. It's been so long since it was like this.

What a few days earlier she'd viewed as a betrayal and an imprisonment, she now saw as a means of unifying the nuclear family. Her parents had divorced more than half her lifetime ago, but now she'd gone to the loony bin and brought everyone together again. Her mania was a blessing in disguise, she said, just the thing to repair the breach between her mother and father, and between them and her siblings.

I didn't have the heart to tell her it wouldn't last.

One night she asked if I would please bring her a map and a book about gardening. I want to look at places far away from here, she said. I want to think about growing things. I want the idea of fresh air. I can't have any here. They won't let me leave. Not even for five minutes.

The next night I brought her a guide to flower gardening and a Rand McNally atlas. She set them aside without looking at them.

During her second week at Mount Sinai, I fell ill with a foul winter cold. I called in sick to work and didn't leave my bed for three days. I'd never been so thankful to feel so bad; it meant I didn't have to sit in her sterile room and pretend I was still her boyfriend.

The morning she checked out, her father dropped her off at my place with a prescription bag full of pill bottles. After a few minutes of bogus pleasantries he fled, as I'd figured he would.

I tended to Rachel with cool solicitude, clinical courtesy. She shone with a glittering confusion, beautiful and fragile as a Fabergé egg. That fragility haunted me. Our relationship had been best when we'd offered each other pleasure with our minds and bodies on a plane of equals. I had no sense that she wanted me anymore, only that she needed me, and it was precisely that neediness, so uncharacteristic of her, that made me want to flee. If I truly wanted to learn the art of taking care, here was my chance—but to be needed by someone was more than I could stand, because I knew I would fail. I just knew.

I get the feeling I'm becoming a burden on you, she said on the third day.

This isn't the easiest thing I've ever done. I'm not sure who you are anymore.

She looked at me with a mixture of surprise and disdain.

I think I need some time at home, she said. I've been away too long.

Those words were the sweetest music I'd heard in weeks. Maybe if her father had whisked her away to the country for a month, my fear would have passed and we'd have made it. But I knew it was over and I knew I was a bastard for being grateful it was over. And as long as it was truly over I could live with being a bastard. I'd lived with worse.

That afternoon she left for Virginia. That evening I called the phone sex line.

It felt like coming home.

PART THREE

Falling Man

One might think an institution that existed to chronicle the story of American capitalism would be uniquely prepared for a fluctuation in the business cycle, but Dow Jones & Company had made a number of blunders that left it ill-prepared for tough times. To give but the most glaring example: In the late 1980s, the company bought ever-increasing shares of an electronic provider of business information called Telerate, for a final total of $1.6 billion. It was meant to compete with Reuters and Bloomberg. A decade later, Dow Jones dumped Telerate at a loss of more than a billion dollars, and no one ever heard of it afterward. The "new economy" bubble was a fiction that allowed the company to believe it might recover from the shocks of Telerate and other poor decisions, but the sudden implosion of tech stocks in 2000 hit Dow Jones like a blow to the solar plexus. Ad revenue tanked. Managers at the flagship editorial product in the universe of Dow Jones brands were instructed to streamline their budgets.

In the spring of 2001 we received a memo announcing company-wide layoffs. Two months later another memo appeared in our in-boxes, announcing further staff reductions. The memos kept coming. In July we received one informing us that the indoor plants would no longer be maintained throughout our offices—for a total savings of $40,000 a year. Reporters and editors were urged to pick a plant to babysit if we wished to see it stay, or, failing that, adopt one and take it home. Rumors began to circulate that the company would be sold to a competitor—the *New York Times*, the *Washington Post*. In the office cafeteria, reporters and editors had the hangdog look of a dwindling tribe being hunted by enemies with superior weaponry.

That summer I scheduled a trip to New Mexico, while I still possessed the benefit of paid vacations. It was less vacation, though, than reporting mission. I wanted to see the public records on Dan's death. After years spent imagining and reimagining the scene of his end, I'd finally made peace with the fact that his suicide was the only story that really interested me.

Trouble was, my stance of ambiguity toward it now felt phony; I didn't know him at all, never really had, probably never would, and what I called ambiguity was just a convenient cover for my ignorance. My mistake, I belatedly realized, was to so fixate on his death that I lost contact with who he'd been in life. The darkness of the act of suicide, the violence of it, the despair it bespoke, the raised middle finger it offered to the world—all that blotted out whatever he'd been while he lived. I couldn't access him. Too many questions; too few answers. A yawning silence, a black hole: that's what he'd become, more symbol than flesh.

It was time, at long last, to confront the carnage head-on, to replace all the horrific images of my own devising with the cold, clinical truth. It was time to start at the end and see if I could work backward into his life. Seidel had suggested this in one of his poems, in lines I felt were aimed straight at me: *To start at End / And work back / To the Mouth / Is the start—*. He had all the answers, it seemed, for the questions that gripped me just then. *The best way not to kill yourself / Is to ride a motorcycle very fast. / How to avoid suicide? / Get on and really ride.* I didn't have a motorcycle but I secured a rental car and took it for a spin on the interstate south of Albuquerque, out beyond Belen, pushing the needle into triple digits. All the while I thought of what I'd find in the files.

That night in my hotel I thought too of my little sister and how she'd reacted in the immediate aftermath of Dan's suicide. Lisa and I shared a similar calm exterior, an inscrutable demeanor that left our true feelings a mystery to those around us—even, on occasion, to each other. On the day Dan's body had arrived on a plane from New Mexico, to be driven from Minneapolis to the town in southern Minnesota where our parents lived, Lisa had slipped away unnoticed and paid a visit to Almlie Funeral Home. She told Mr. Almlie that she wanted to view the body. She wanted, for her own peace of mind, to say goodbye in person.

Almlie hesitated before he replied. He understood, he said. He'd probably even feel the same way if he were in her shoes. But the decision to have a closed-casket funeral had been made for good reason.

I don't care, she said, I need to see him.

He tried to dissuade her. She wouldn't back down. And so he told her that when he'd finished preparing the body, she could have her wish. He needed a few hours. He'd give her a signal. When he turned on the light above the front door of the funeral home she could enter, but not before. In this way he could honor her request to avoid calling her at our parents' house and arousing their suspicion. Around nine-thirty or ten o'clock, he said. I should be finished by then.

He paused again, thinking.

Can you identify him by his hands?

Yes, she said.

Beginning around nine-thirty she drove back and forth along the street in front of the funeral home. Fifteen minutes passed, a half hour. She began to think he might go back on his word, or she'd missed his signal and he'd gone home for the night. She parked her car across the street and waited with the radio playing softly, waited what seemed an eternity.

When the light came on, Almlie led her to a room where the coffin stretched against the back wall. The two portions of its lid were open, but the head of the corpse was covered by a cloth. Lisa stepped forward and looked at the pair of hands folded across an unmoving torso. She noted the fine red hair between the knuckles.

Would you mind if I had a little time alone with him? she asked.

He nodded and backed away.

She waited until his footsteps faded down the hallway. When she was sure he was gone, she lifted the cloth to reveal his head. Her first feeling was one of relief that his face was there at all—a conjecture had floated through our extended family that the force of the gunshot had blown it away. His eyes, however, had been removed, the sockets sewn shut. At his right temple was a neat hole the size of a dime, on the left side of his head a much larger hole whose size she did not quantify, only to say that it convinced her he had not suffered, that his death had been instantaneous.

She took a pair of scissors from her pocket and discreetly cut a lock of his hair to give to our mother. She unfolded the cloth and tucked it back in place. She pulled from her purse a letter she'd written him and placed it in the pocket of his blazer, taking care it didn't protrude and invite attention. She whispered a few final words—I never asked her what she'd said, or what she'd written, and she never volunteered to share—and then she called Almlie back in the room.

When Lisa told me all this, late on the night it happened, I was torn between admiration and jealousy. Admiration for her courage, certainly—a nineteen-year-old woman, nervy as can be in the face of her brother's ugly death—but also an irrational jealousy at how insistent was her desire to pay last respects. I wondered whether she thought of this act of visitation as a burden she was best equipped to carry, and knowing this she decided to carry it alone; I suspected as much. That was the little sister I'd always known, unafraid of doing what was hard if she thought it was right, with no need for a pat on the back, and no interest in philosophizing about what it meant.

I was jealous, I realized, because I hadn't thought of it

myself. I wondered if it would have made a difference to have seen him in the flesh one last time, to have looked his deed in the face and not just metaphorically, to have told him what I secretly thought of him before he went underground. Maybe. Maybe not. It was too late to find out.

After a lousy night's sleep in a Motel 6 near the airport, I set out in the morning for the Albuquerque Police Department and the state Office of Medical Investigators, each of which, I'd learned, possessed a report on Dan's death. I went first to the police, where a records clerk promptly made copies of the file at fifty cents per page, eight pages in all:

> The decedent was seated on the living room couch which was against the west wall of the living room. An SKS rifle was found to the immediate right of the decedent between his right arm and right leg. The decedent was attired in green shorts and T-shirt. . . . Several pieces of skull fragments, brain matter and high velocity blood spatter were found throughout the lower level of the apartment. . . .

Later in the report the officer wrote, *I took overall photos of the apartment, exterior and interior.* I asked the clerk if I was entitled to copies of the photos, and she directed me to an office on the second floor called Criminalistics, where I was told the photo lab needed three days to process my order. The photos would be sent to me by mail and arrive in a week to ten days.

Twenty minutes later, on a satellite campus of the University of New Mexico, two men greeted me at the Office of Medical Investigators, the records manager and the doctor who'd performed the autopsy. I'd called ahead to have them pull the file. The records manager was a tall, bearded, solemn, soft-spoken man named Walt, while the medical examiner, Marcus, was genial to the point of oddity, smiling at me, head tilted jauntily, while speaking of the finer points of cranial disfigurement. Walt handed me the autopsy report. I asked him if photos were an additional part of the file, and he said that more than likely they had photos in their archive, unless they were misplaced or damaged in the developing. He promised to check for me and said that if they existed, I did have a right to see them or have them copied. He could mail them to me, in fact.

Marcus grimaced at the thought.

I personally think it's much better if you sit down with us here and allow us to explain what you're seeing, he said. The images, from my reading of the report—and I confess I don't remember this particular case—but the images will likely be very graphic. I'd feel more comfortable showing them to you here than putting them in the mail and having them arrive one day in your mailbox. If you see them and you still want copies, we'll be happy to have them made and sent to you.

Walt consulted his photo archivist. It turned out the photos were readily accessible, so I agreed to return in two hours for a viewing.

Afternoon cumuli had begun to sprout like enormous

white mushrooms over the peaks of the Sandias. The temperature in the valley edged toward one hundred. My palm made a sweaty print on the manila envelope containing the autopsy report. As I walked across campus I felt no urge to open it. My purpose did not demand haste. I wasn't on a deadline. The freshness of the evidence wasn't at issue. There was no criminal who at any moment might strike again, no victim in dire need of justice.

I found my way to an asphalt basketball court in the middle of campus. I asked around and learned the circulation desk at the library kept a ball it allowed to be checked out like a book, as long as you left an ID. I dribbled along the sidewalk toward the court. My veins quivered with adrenaline. I began the routine I'd developed as a teenager dreaming of making varsity: a couple of hard runs at the basket, left-hand layup then right, a few short jumpers, little five- and eight-footers kissed off the board, then some turnaround fadeaways from the baseline. Legs limbering and sweat beginning to flow, I drifted out beyond the three-point line, working my way around it right to left, squaring my shoulders before I shot, chasing down the rebound and spinning the ball out in front of me as I sprinted back toward the arc, where I caught the ball and turned, made a quick fake, and stepped one step left or right before leaping and following through, releasing at the apex of the jump, the seams in the ball perpendicular to my fingers—a habit of the purest shooters, the gym rats with an aesthetic devotion to the pretty arc and spin of the perfect jump shot. I was deep inside a trance of fingertip and follow-through and ball and net, the world reduced to a set of internalized geometries, when a tall, broad-shouldered Native American man sauntered onto the court, snared a rebound in his huge hands, and took a shot, banking it in from ten feet out. He wore jeans and a sweaty tank top and had a slightly forward-leaning posture of defiance.

You got a nice shot, he said.

Thanks. You too.

I played some.

Me too. Long time ago.

He laughed and said, I know how it is.

We circled and shot with unspoken playground etiquette, one man rebounding, the other shooting, the shooter entitled to at least five shots and as many beyond that as he could make in a row, the roles switching when the shooter missed. Within twelve feet he was deadly. He always shot while moving to his right. He didn't dribble well with his left hand. I noticed these things in anticipation of the question he asked a few minutes later, after he'd curled his arm around the ball and wiped the sweat from his brow.

Wanna go one-on-one?

Sure, I said.

Shoot for ball?

Sure. Make-it-take-it to eleven, win by two?

He nodded and took off his shirt. His free throw bounced off the back rim. Mine touched nothing but net. I stepped out beyond the three-point arc. He rolled the ball to me as if it were a bowling ball. I bent to pick it up. He gave me a five-foot cushion, daring me to shoot from where I stood.

He'll learn soon enough, I thought, as I lofted a shot toward the rim.

One-zero, I said.

You like that shot, huh?

I'll take it if you give it to me.

He rolled the ball toward my feet again, a small taunt, a gesture of disrespect meant to annoy me. I didn't hesitate this time. I lifted the ball from the asphalt and cocked it above my shoulder and bent at the knees and rose and shot, one fluid motion that lasted half a second.

Two-zero, I said.

He slapped the ball between his hands and mumbled something I couldn't hear.

Outwardly I projected an air of utter placidity but in my head I talked a silent stream of trash. *You don't want to set up in my face? I'm gonna shoot you down without breaking a sweat. You're not even going to get a shot off before it's over. I'm gonna blank your ass. Eleven-zip, motherfucker.*

He bounced the ball to me this time, a token of begrudging respect. I caught it and shot again in a single coiled stroke. He leaped toward me, stretching to block or tip the shot, but he was late by a fraction of a second.

Three-zero.

The freebies were over. He knew he couldn't give me space. He didn't bounce or roll the ball, he handed it over from arm's length. He crowded me and waved his hands in my face. I dribbled backward a couple of steps, slowly, nonchalantly, and when he started moving toward me, his momentum carrying him away from the basket, I made a quick crossover dribble, left to right, and blew past him toward the hoop.

When I'd finished whipping him and we'd shaken hands, we sat in the shade of some trees and shared water from his jug. He said his name was Raymond. I asked him about his job on the campus grounds crew. He'd been doing the same few things every day for five summers now: mowing, trimming trees and bushes, inspecting and maintaining the sprinkler system. Today he'd been repairing a valve in a water line and merely wanted to prolong his break, divert his mind from the boredom of his work. He thanked me for playing with him, shook my hand again very intently, called me a worthy foe.

I wasn't so sure. There could be no good reason for the fierceness with which I'd beaten the poor man—unless I'd unconsciously made him a stand-in for my brother, the brother I'd always begged to shoot hoops with me when we were kids, the brother whose corpse was described in painstaking detail in the soggy manila envelope at my feet.

After Raymond left, I sat for a while and read.

The body is received clad in an olive green T-shirt which is blood-stained in the back, an olive green pair of shorts, two white socks and one pair of blue undershorts.

The body is cool to touch. Rigor mortis is fully fixed. Fixed purple livor mortis extends over the dorsal surfaces of the body, except in areas exposed to pressure.

The scalp hair is red and measures 3 inches in length over the crown. The irises are hazel. The pupils are bilaterally equal at 0.6 cm. The cornea are translucent. The sclerae and conjunctivae are unremarkable. The nose and ears are not unusual. The decedent wears a 1/2 inch red mustache and beard. The teeth are natural and in good repair. The neck is unremarkable.

The thorax is well-developed and symmetrical. The abdomen is flat. The anus and back are unremarkable.

The penis is circumcised. The testes are bilaterally descended within the scrotum.

The upper and lower extremities are well-developed and symmetrical, without absence of digits.

No identifying marks or scars are readily apparent.

There is no evidence of medical intervention.

I returned the basketball, retrieved my driver's license, and walked across the grounds to the Office of Medical Investigators.

Walt and Marcus ushered me into a bland conference room equipped with a slide projector and a pull-down screen. First Marcus offered explanations for some of the more technical language in the autopsy report. "Distorted calvarium," for instance, meant that part of Dan's skull had collapsed from the force of the bullet. Marcus again warned me about the gruesomeness of what I was about to see. I swiveled in my chair and faced the screen.

Are you ready? Marcus asked.

Yes, I'm ready, I said.

Walt turned out the lights.

The image projected to the screen was more horrific than any I'd imagined, and over the years I'd imagined a lot. I'd expected a grainy black-and-white snapshot, but the color saturation was as lush as a tropical sunset, the reds as vibrant as the seeds of a pomegranate. A giant chunk of the left side of his head was gone. His left eye and ear were still intact, but barely—above them was a gaping red cavity where his brain used to be. A piece of skull appeared to hang as if on a hinge from the top of his head, and what remained of his right forehead was crumpled inward. His eyes stared implacably at the camera, and his mouth hung ajar, as if he'd been in the middle of saying something when he pulled the trigger. The doctor showed several more pictures, some of them close-ups of the entrance and exit wounds, but it was the first that stayed with me—the force of the bullet evident in all its ferocity, the visual confirmation of the laconic language in the report: *Portions of the cerebral hemisphere are submitted in a separate plastic bag.*

Not surprisingly, Seidel had seen it all in advance:

The wind lifts off his face,
Which flutters
In the wind and snaps back and forth,
Just barely attached.

It smiles horribly—
A flag flapping on a flagpole.

I took copies of the photos, thanked the two men, and headed north for the backcountry of Bandelier National Monument, where for three days I did something I hadn't done since my time in Montana. I lived in silence, in the out of doors, moving through mesa country with a pack on my back past no more evidence of human life than adobe ruins and scattered potsherds, lost in a tactile world of stone and wood and clay, sleeping beneath the stars in a land as foreign to me as the moon. I didn't see a soul. I didn't want to leave. But duty called.

I'd been back in New York for two weeks when I came home from work one night and found a fat envelope in my mailbox. The return address—Albuquerque Police Department, Criminalistics Division, Forensic Photography Unit— warned me what I'd find inside.

I poured myself a glass of bourbon and sat with it, turned it in my hand, sipping now and then, savoring the smoky burn, telling myself there was nothing to fear. He was dead. The documentation wouldn't change a thing that mattered.

I finished the glass of bourbon and poured myself another and then I opened the envelope.

Among the images it contained—a photo from the front of his apartment, down the long hallway to his living room, a slumped body faintly visible on the couch in the corner; a photo taken from partway down the hallway, the slumped body now more prominent, pale arms, pale legs showing through the gloom; a photo of his bedroom, two white cowboy hats upside down on the bed, as if he'd tried them on and tossed them aside; a photo of his kitchen counter, coffeemaker on the left of the frame, a hunk of bloody viscera pooled next to it, twenty feet from the body; a photo of the wall above the couch, spattered with blood and yellowish bits of brain matter; another like it from another angle, and another like it, and another like it; a photo of his body from above, right arm pointed downward, left arm bent at the elbow, gun cradled between them at an angle, stock resting on the floor next to his right leg, barrel pointed toward his left shoulder; a photo still closer of just his head, eyes open as if in shock, portions of his skull peeled back from the force of the bullet, the entire left side of his head all red and wet like a watermelon crushed with a baseball bat; a photo of a big chunk of his brain, disgorged but still intact, lying next to him on the couch all glistening and salmon-colored, like a skinned cat; a photo of a bullet hole in the ceiling; a photo of a rifle cartridge on the floor, nestled in the carpet; a photo of a box of cartridges on the floor, PMC brand, prominently stamped with the words WARNING: KEEP OUT OF THE REACH OF CHILDREN—I came across a photo of his left foot, clad in a white ankle sock, and next to it the telephone, its cord pulled taut across the room, its keypad stippled with a mist of blood.

That was the one I couldn't get past.

I put down the photos and picked up the bottle.

For weeks afterward I walked the night streets of the

city, caressing the bitter estrangement of my secret knowledge, my glimpse at the tableau of his end. I drank myself into furious oblivion, alone in my new neighborhood bar at closing time, and in the morning I stared at a blank piece of paper in the typewriter before I dressed for work.

I should have called him. I could have called him. That's what I kept thinking, staring at that empty page. I should have called him. I could have called him. My mother had suggested as much, and I'd put it off. I'd figured it could wait. The sight of that telephone in the police photos only confirmed my conviction that I'd had a chance to save him and missed it. There was no way around it. The phone was right there, within arm's reach. Its ringing could have changed the course of his day. My voice could have given him a reason to live. I'd never have known it, of course. Hard to imagine him saying, months later, *So, bro, that time you called me after the breakup . . . you saved my life.*

Instead he was gone, still and forever gone.

I spoke to Bob Bartley for the last time on the day he announced his retirement as editorial page editor. Dow Jones & Company required senior executives to retire at the age of sixty-five, so Bob Bartley would be replaced as editorial page editor by Paul Gigot, who'd won a Pulitzer Prize for commentary and often appeared on *The MacNeil/ Lehrer NewsHour* on PBS. Bob Bartley would still write a weekly column called Thinking Things Over, in which he would say the same things he'd been thinking for thirty years all over again.

We boarded the elevator together, just the two of us. His hair was mussed, and his shoulders were slumped. He had the doleful look of an injured horse aware it's about to be taken out to pasture and shot.

Big day, I said, trying to sound jocular.

Yes, he said.

Now Paul gets to see how hard you work, I said, staying jocular.

That's right, he said. And I have to figure out how to disengage. Not sure how to do that. Maybe stop coming into the office every day.

Yes, I can imagine that would be a challenge after thirty years.

He didn't respond.

I tried to think of something else to say to him—something big-picture or consequential, now that his reign was up. I thought of asking him how he felt about an in-depth study of his editorials by the *Columbia Journalism Review*, which found that his page "rarely offers balance, is often unfair, and is riddled with errors—distortions and outright falsehoods of every kind and stripe." I thought too of asking him whether he felt in any way responsible for the death of Vincent Foster, the White House counsel to Bill Clinton who'd killed himself shortly after Bob Bartley published a series of attacks on his integrity. Foster's suicide note, discovered in his briefcase six days after police found his body in a suburban Washington park, expressed frustration that "the WSJ editors lie without consequence." After Foster's death, Bob Bartley's editorials insinuated that Foster may have been murdered for knowing too much about Whitewater, and called for a special counsel to investigate. "The American public is entitled to know if Mr. Foster's death was somehow connected to his high office," Bob Bartley wrote. I thought the American public was entitled to know if Bob Bartley thought Vince Foster's suicide was somehow connected to irresponsible journalism, and I wondered whether Bob Bartley had considered, for even a moment, the family of the dead man when he wrote those words. They made it difficult to think of Bob Bartley as a man who no doubt loved his wife and kids, was generous with colleagues, tithed the appropriate amount at his church of choice, and did kind things for his friends. Though I detested his politics, it was this sin that disfigured him so grotesquely, turned him into a caricature of a human being in my mind, an obsession I would even dare say: that nothing was off-limits in the pursuit of a political vendetta, including paranoid musings on a man's tragic suicide.

In my heart I knew it was the wrong day for such questions, and anyway I was a coward when it came to asking tough questions of anyone but myself, and even often of myself—one of the reasons I knew I wasn't cut out to be a reporter.

We parted ways in the lobby, him heading for his limousine to Brooklyn, me for the subway to Queens.

Well, I said, enjoy your newfound freedom.

I'll try, he said.

I never spoke to him again.

....

I held mornings sacred, time entirely my own, in my own space, with my own music on the stereo. Alone in my bed I'd wake to the alarm and the day's first light, make a pot of coffee. A hot shower and a shave, a shirt, a tie. An hour at the typewriter, coffee at hand, jabbing the machine to make a sound like a thing being built. I wrote and rewrote the story of my brother's end that summer, based on what I'd once been told by my aunt Ruth, who'd spoken to all the principals. It was the one story that never got old in the revision. I'd compile new versions, new variations, improvisations on a tune I couldn't quite seem to hear; I'd give it a rest when the versions started changing one word at a time instead of blossoming in new directions. Then I'd strip away anything extraneous, cut it to the bone, aiming for the very minimum I could say for certain plus a little I could not. I wanted to fashion an ice pick out of words. I wanted concision, dispassion, an accurate accounting of a man's last moves on the brink of a self-willed death. Despite my best effort, I couldn't help thinking it stylized and incomplete:

He spent his last afternoon with friends, this much was known. One of them had a hot tub. They soaked and drank beer and told stories and laughed. They were all hot air balloonists, and their stories tended to circle around dubious flying conditions, botched landings, hairy takeoffs in squirrelly winds.

The afternoon passed toward evening. Someone suggested they go out for a drink, to a neighborhood place they liked in Rio Rancho, a place called Phil's Bar. Dan said he wanted to go home and get his darts so he could play some cricket. Seven o'clock, it was agreed. They'd meet at seven. They'd see him then.

Back in his apartment, he picked up the telephone and dialed his ex-girlfriend. She'd been his girlfriend for eight months, his ex since the previous day. She had two kids, a boy and a girl, with a man from whom she was separated, not divorced. The kids were ages seven and eleven and both had begun to dress in a cowboy hat and boots, in imitation of Dan. Final custody remained uncertain, property yet to be divided, papers yet to be signed. It was a messy situation, and Wendy had insisted on a break while she got her life in order. A break and then they'd see where things stood.

He was drunk when he called. They spoke briefly, talking past each other, saying things they didn't mean, as sundered lovers will.

You're not thinking straight, she told him. Sleep it off. Call me tomorrow.

This was his last known contact with another human voice.

From then on it's all conjecture. Maybe he went to the couch with his lowball glass, working it around in his hand, swirling the ice, not even noticing the taste when he drank. Maybe he couldn't sit still. Maybe he was up and pacing the apartment. Maybe he was thinking that the only thing to do was hurt her back. Maybe he was thinking that the only thing to do was hurt himself.

He stepped out on his deck for some fresh air. Or maybe he went again to the freezer, put another chunk of ice in his glass, poured himself another finger of scotch. Or maybe he opened a beer. He paced from one room to the next. Or maybe he sat on the couch and worked the glass around in his hand some more.

There it is, he thought. Right there, behind the closet door, the answer for everything.

He opened the closet. He reached for the gun. He felt the barrel, smooth cool metal. Maybe he caressed it with a kind of loving tenderness. Maybe he simply connected the clip, snapped it in place with a grim satisfaction. He drank a long swallow of scotch. Or maybe he cracked another beer. He walked from one end of the apartment to the other, brandishing the gun, getting a feel for it. Or maybe he sat and tested it against his temple, savoring the chill of it on his skin, testing the membrane between life and death. Maybe he leaned into it, relieved by the onrushing prospect of freedom. Maybe he was calm. Maybe he took his time. Maybe he was itching to get it over. Maybe he was furious. Maybe he felt as if his head were entrapped in a goldfish bowl. There was no one else in his diminishing world, nothing but the vise grip of despair, squeezing him without mercy, reducing his options for escape to the flash from the mouth of the gun.

. . . .

This was my continuing dream that summer, the locus for my imagination, a voyeuristic wish to inhabit the scene of a suicide, to see the carnage firsthand and taste the smoke in the air, the smoke from the heat of the bullet.

My commute, door to door, typically took fifty minutes on the N train. It was another part of my day I cherished, a three-quarter-hour journey in benevolent captivity, an in-between time. On the train I came back to the world outside my own head. Boarding near the end of the line, before the cars became crowded, I usually managed to find a place to sit. I used the time to read or, when my attention faltered, to survey the kaleidoscope of city life in the faces of my fellow New Yorkers, the galvanic friction of young and old, rich and poor, black and white and every shade between. Bound in a fragile intimacy sustained through studied nonchalance, we were acutely aware of those near us but discreet with our attentions lest we send a creeper vibe, most of us anyway. There were always creepers and I tried not to be one of them. Nonetheless about every other day I swooned for a woman I would never see again, a one-way romance consummated in a sideways glance and lasting mere minutes, poignant in its transience and futility, in the sickly purity of my unexpressed longing.

I had one commute more memorable than all others by far. It was election day, the mayoral primary—a day on which the city painted itself in red, white, and blue, posters and placards taped to light poles and subway-stop railings, an upbeat but languid mood in the streets, as people played hooky from work to do their civic duty. I intended to vote in the evening at my polling place in Queens, for Mark Green, whom I felt sure would be the city's next mayor if he survived Fernando Ferrer.

As it happened, neither man would be much heard from again.

At a little after nine a.m. my telephone rang. It startled me. No one ever called me in the morning. I had a bad feeling before I even answered.

My friend Sarah wanted to know if I'd heard the news. I told her I hadn't heard any news. She said two planes had hit the World Trade Center towers. It looked like terrorism.

You probably won't be going to work today, she said.

Damned if I won't, I thought.

On my way to the subway, having just missed a train pulling out of the station, I stopped in a bar and looked at the television, saw the two towers framed by the camera, both of them smoking, not white smoke but black, a hint of the tremendous heat at work. It looked bad, but I couldn't begin to imagine how bad. I made a vow that sustained me through the next three hours of travel by train and by foot to an office building I would enter for what would turn out to be the last time: I would not be reduced to a stunned spectator. I would not sit in a bar and stare at a screen. This was the biggest story in the world all of a sudden, and it was happening just across the street from my employer, a newspaper regarded as a secular bible by some of the people who worked in those towers. I didn't care what I had to do, I was going to work, straight to the managing editor, to whom I'd offer myself for whatever was needed, phone dictation, rewrite, you name it. It was strange to feel this way—preemptively purposeful. I'd become so jaded with the limitations of journalism that I no longer thought of myself as a journalist but as merely another drone in the hive mind of Lower Manhattan, trading eight hours of each weekday for cash at a paper whose editorial stance I found not just wrong but dangerous. Some habits die hard, I guess. I'd spent seven years, off and on, and many tens of thousands of dollars on an education that taught me three major things: stay curious, be dogged, run toward the story. Old instincts kicked in like a muscle memory.

So I went to the story, which turned out to be many stories, depending on how you looked at it: a heinous crime, an audacious act of mass murder, a made-for-TV spectacle, a catastrophic fire, an airborne toxic event, and the most successful terrorist attack in the history of terrorism. September 11 was a lot of things and the beginning of many more: refugees and civilian dead in foreign lands, killed and wounded soldiers, TSA gropings, the Patriot Act, extraordinary rendition, CIA black sites, waterboarding, a linguistic squabble disguising a moral question about the meaning of the word torture, the prison at Guantánamo Bay, sadomasochistic photo shoots at Abu Ghraib, Total Information Awareness, drone assassinations, border hysteria, NSA data collection . . . a full accounting is beyond my ken. But before all that, before it became a rallying cry for war and state surveillance, it was a drama of suicide. Nineteen men on a mission demanding death on a day chosen for them. An untold number of jumpers from the towers who faced a choice of deaths on a day not chosen by them. A chain reaction of suicides. The hijackers believed their reward awaited them in the afterlife. The jumpers, who can say what they believed? When it came to the afterlife, they must have believed dozens of different things, but the one thing they all believed was that ten final seconds of flight was preferable to the inferno they fled.

Later I tried to imagine their final moments, as I had with my brother's, but how far inside another man's death can we truly see? Even our own is a mystery until it's upon us, and for the people in those towers it can only be guessed at in the most superficial way. The thunderous explosion from the impact of the plane. Instantaneous fire erupting with a searing heat, the fire quickly growing. Panic as all exits close off. Smoke and flames swallowing all hope of survival, breathing excruciating, lungs overwhelmed. Suffocate or roast to death or jump, those were the choices, the last set of options, the question of how to die. There wasn't much time to mull it over. It wasn't a philosophical exercise. Die now—but die how? It was a question whose horror you couldn't inhabit.

I was always ending up in all the wrong places: Bed-Stuy, the *Wall Street Journal*, the make-believe province of telephonic copulation. In order not to feel satisfied with life in the wake of my brother's death—in order to prove to myself that I had loved him—I'd denied myself contentment in all its forms, as if pleasure were anathema to my holy grief. In an orderly world I'd have had no business working across the street from those towers, a pig farmer's son from Minnesota, graduate of the University of Montana, a country boy in every way that mattered, though I'd tried to pretend otherwise. I had no business at all living in New York City, a place I'd judged hostile to most of what was beautiful about life on earth when I first encountered it. An arts page copy editor, I certainly had no business staring into the center of the biggest story in the world on a late summer day, rubbing my eyes, snapping pictures with a digital camera, inhaling pulverized asbestos, burning plastic, burning metal, burning paper, burning fuel, burning flesh. The images I encountered that day were ghastly, a scene of destruction on a scale unimaginable even as I stood on the edge of it, but it was the smell that stayed with me, remains with me to this day: the smell of an airplane made into a bullet.

By an accident of fate I finally got my wish. I paid witness in the flesh to the scene of a suicide—countless suicides. There was nothing else to do. The office was empty when I got there. The whole building was empty, evacuated hours before. I climbed the fire stairs and walked around the newsroom, amazed to find myself alone at lunchtime on a weekday, in a workplace typically restless with several hundred people living in the perpetual now of gathering news. When it finally sank in that I was useless, I went back outside and stood on the edge of the smoking rubble, trying and failing to understand what had happened, a spectator minus the distancing screen. Paper blanketed the ash that blanketed the streets. Firefighters sat stunned, covered in dust, their heads in their hands. There was nowhere to look and not find evidence of ruin. I joined a group of five reporters at the southwest edge of the pile. Two of them scribbled in notebooks. One fiddled with a tape recorder. One snapped pictures, one held a video camera. No one said a word that was printable in a family newspaper.

When the smoke made my lungs clench with intimations of an asthma attack, I walked north until I found a city bus. I sat down next to a man who told me he'd evacuated the north tower, and on his way down he'd walked past dozens of firefighters headed up. They're gone, he said. They have to be, every one of them. I remember the faces. I don't think I'll ever forget.

I got off the bus at McHale's, dusted in ash to the knees, but the usual discretion ruled. On me, the barkeep said, as she poured my first drink. No one asked me where I'd been. No one needed to. All eyes were on the television; I watched for a while and then I caught a taxi home.

The next day's *Wall Street Journal* was produced that night in New Jersey and carried a six-column headline in type nearly as large as the masthead, the fourth banner headline in the paper's history:

> *Terrorists Destroy World Trade Center,*
> *Hit Pentagon in Raid with Hijacked Jets*

I bought it and a copy of the *Times* at my corner newsstand early on the morning of September 12. I read all the front page stories and most of the inside of both papers, but one simple photo on page A7 of the *Times* stopped me cold. Taken by an Associated Press photographer, it showed a man in midflight. His head was down, his torso parallel to the vertical ribbing of the two towers behind him, several stories of them that filled the frame to the edge. He appeared to be falling along the demarcation line between them. One leg was straight, the other bent at ninety degrees. Together they formed a little triangle. One of his boots stood out, starkly black. His pants were black, his shirt white. His arms appeared relaxed. He looked almost peaceful, like a man suspended on a string, even as he hurtled with accelerating speed. His was the emblematic image of the terror of that day, though afterward it was not much seen again in the world of American journalism. We airbrushed him from the record. Readers excoriated the papers that published the photo, and the papers scrubbed it from their Web sites. We couldn't bear to think of the panic of his final moments, his awful need for flight. We wanted pictures of heroism, patriotism—firemen or flags, or better yet firemen holding flags—and he did not fit the bill. He was the incarnation of our last taboo, the avatar of our worst private nightmare, a human being captured in the act of a self-willed death.

Only Connect

After the attacks we commuted to the cornfields of New Jersey, a trip that took me two hours one way. We put the paper together in a makeshift newsroom in the training wing of Dow Jones corporate headquarters near Princeton. Almost all the stories in the paper concerned terrorism: its practitioners, finances, backers, tactics, goals. It felt, for a time, a little embarrassing to edit pieces about the Cave of Altamira or an Ansel Adams show.

When anthrax turned up in the offices of other media companies, all of our mail underwent a heat-steam treatment. The mailroom workers sorted it with masks on their faces and rubber gloves on their hands. They looked like lab technicians working with a deadly poison. When opened, the envelopes crackled like dead leaves, and the ink on the letters was often illegible.

On the editorial page the imprint of Bob Bartley lingered, his obsessions trotted out for endless encores: the beneficence of tax cuts, the imperative of a missile defense system, the need for military spending on hardware and troops for vast overseas mobilization. Saddam Hussein became an urgent addition to the repertoire; Osama bin Laden appeared as an afterthought. I started keeping a folder of clippings, called FULL BLOWN INSANITY ON THE WSJ EDITORIAL PAGE.

On September 12 the lead editorial stated: "We are entitled to presume that this is the work of the usual suspects—Saddam Hussein, the Taliban, the Iranian mullahs and other dictators who invoke Muslim fundamentalism to justify their fundamentally illegitimate power." There was no mention of what made the authorial we entitled to such a wide-ranging presumption, nor was there mention of the man who turned out to be the mastermind of the attacks. The next day his name snuck into print alongside the primary suspect: "We would not be surprised if this week's atrocity was the work of Saddam or bin Laden or both." This contention was driven home by the pull quote in the adjacent opinion piece: "Can Osama bin Laden sow terror alone? Not likely. His group has had help from Saddam Hussein, and from Sudan."

The next day the lead editorial called for hastening deployment of a missile-defense shield—"missile defense is as much a defense against hijacked airliners as it is against missiles," it stated bizarrely—an effort that seemed to me like a man lifting an umbrella over his head while being pelted in the groin by snowballs.

On September 19, an unsigned editorial argued that the first and most important steps in combatting terrorism ought to include capital-gains tax cuts and immediate drilling for oil in Alaska. The same editorial stated: "Throughout history the periods of greatest military innovation have been wars. Now is the time to push for next-generation weaponry and electronics that will keep the U.S. ahead of not just terrorists but all adversaries. Democracies are reluctant to spend money on defense in peacetime, but in a war they will give the military whatever it needs." It would seem that war was needed, because a massive military buildup was needed, because nineteen men with box cutters had flown passenger jets into three iconic buildings on American soil. I couldn't follow the logic but I knew they wouldn't stop clamoring until they got themselves an honest-to-god, maim-and-kill war.

Reading the paper became an exercise in cognitive dissonance. One day the news section would report that "U.S. Officials Discount Any Role by Iraq in Terrorist Attacks," quoting intelligence officials who noted that bin Laden disliked Saddam and the two had nothing in common but a hatred for America; the next day the editorial page would write that "reports are swirling that Saddam Hussein was also behind last week's attacks. . . . Deposing Saddam has to be considered another war aim."

In this rank potpourri of erroneous speculation, dubious reasoning, and calculated propaganda, about the only thing in the back pages of the A section that felt true was Seidel's monthly poem. All the opinion columns calling for "total war," targeted assassinations, the bombing of madrassas, and the American occupation of countries as diverse as Afghanistan, Iraq, Sudan, Libya, Iran, and Syria—"The Answer to Terrorism? Colonialism," a headline proposed a month after the attacks—all of it seemed unhinged and delusional next to eight stanzas of Seidel's verse, which, by adopting a voice as twisted and chilling as that of Osama bin Laden, seemed to get much closer to the heart of the matter.

> I like the color of the smell. I like the odor of spoiled meat.
> I like how gangrene transubstantiates warm firm flesh into rotten sleet.
> When the blue blackens and they amputate, I fly.
> I am flying a Concorde of modern passengers to gangrene in the sky.

Needless to say, some of the paper's more sensitive readers were not impressed; several wrote letters to the editor calling for Seidel to cease and desist.

Post-attacks, I heard a noticeable increase in traffic on the talk line. I called often with the hope I'd get lucky.

One night I did.

Her greeting was ambiguous, almost shy: *Hi, this is Christine. Just looking for something interesting. . . .* Her voice had a quality of innocence unlike the moaners, the nasty talkers, the men in their girlfriends' lacy underwear.

I pressed two and recorded my Clark Kent Calling from a Phone Booth routine—professional journalist, late twenties, looking for a smart, sexy woman to share bedroom superheroics.

She responded. She laughed and said she liked my voice.

She was a photographer and was intrigued by writers, especially writers with superhero powers. She wondered where I was calling from, where I was from originally. I didn't sound like a native New Yorker. She couldn't place the voice, but it wasn't New York.

We traded polite messages for a few minutes—I lived in Queens, she lived in Manhattan. I was from the Midwest, she was from the South. I was twenty-nine and single, she was thirty-seven and separated from her husband. We shared a taste in music: blues, jazz, country, gospel.

Finally I made the move. I pressed three and recorded my pitch: Hey, listen, you sound really cool and I was hoping you might want to talk directly. I hope so. . . .

Your connection will be arranged shortly. Please hold. . . .

Please hold for a live connection. . . .

We're about to connect you one-on-one with another talk line caller. If you hear a chime, that means another caller has sent you a message. To disconnect from your live chat, just press the star key. Now, prepare to speak to caller number 32.

For a moment I was speechless. I had no idea what she was after, but there was a seductive quality to her voice that made me want to figure it out and give it to her, whatever it might be. Mercifully, she untied my tongue with humor. She teasingly called me Clark and wondered why I wasn't out in the city, saving damsels in distress. She speculated that I was recovering from an encounter with Kryptonite, and when I confessed that, like most superheroes, I was taciturn, not at all a smooth talker, she had great fun with the irony—a not-so-smooth talker on a talk line. Our laughter led to candor, and soon we were exchanging confessions of embarrassment: two urban professionals, not repulsive in any obvious way, reduced to seeking sexual gratification through a telephone line. Maybe my faux-humility charmed her, but all of a sudden she said, Listen, Superman, do you want to come over?

I stammered in reply—*Uh, you mean, uh, now? Tonight?*—and my hesitation must have made her wonder what I'd failed to disclose. The wife? The felony rap? The prosthetic hook for a hand? Because she began to backtrack, saying she'd never done this before, it was crazy, she didn't know me at all, I could be a stalker, some sadistic weirdo.

I suppose I could be, I said. But I'm being honest when I tell you I'm not. I'm a shy boy from a little house on the prairie. I make my bed every morning. I pay my bills on time.

We went around and around like that. Having extended the invitation, she felt a need to explore every single reason it was a bad idea. But I wasn't going to let it slide. I had a hunch I could convince her.

Eventually, I did.

We don't have to do anything, she said. If we don't find each other attractive we can just, I don't know. Talk. Or do nothing. Walk away.

Okay.

Just one thing. What's your real name?

Phil. Is yours Christine?

No. It's Molly.

Molly. I'll see you soon, Molly.

When I came up the stairs she was leaning half out of her doorway, hoping to see me before I saw her. We looked at each other and smiled, a wave of mutual relief—*thank goodness he/she isn't hideous!*—washing over us.

I can't believe I'm doing this, she said.

She wore a white blouse and blue jeans. Her hair was long and curly, the color of cinnamon. Her lips were darkened with fresh lipstick. She looked younger than thirty-seven. Her jeans clung tightly—but not too tightly—to her hips. She'd obviously spent some time—but not too much time—primping for a visitor.

I guess you should come in, she said.

We sat at the kitchen table. A stick of incense smoked in an ashtray. The place looked dramatically uncluttered for a Manhattan apartment. Then I remembered her husband had just moved out, him and all his things.

She set two beers on the table, lit herself a cigarette, offered the pack to me. I wondered how long we would pretend this was a date.

She told me her husband had left two months ago. He'd given no precise reason. He felt them drifting apart, he needed some space, a bunch of vague clichés. At first she was devastated. She hadn't seen it coming. Then he left, and that was it. She was alone. She told herself she'd better get used to it. On September 11, he'd come back and spent the night—*the world is ending, at least we have each other*—but it felt wrong. She indulged him for forty-eight hours because she was fearful too. Then she told him to get out. He said he was ready to try again, but she wasn't. It hurt, goddamn it hurt, but she had to do it. You don't just walk out on a marriage and walk back in when the world makes you scared to be alone. It couldn't be the same, not after what he'd done. He now held all the power—*I want to go, I want to stay, I want I want I want.* She couldn't let him have that. She couldn't let him have that and still respect herself. She knew that if she let him back in she'd live in constant fear of the next departure, the final departure, and she knew the fear would disfigure her, make her crazy with dread.

Seventeen years! she said, shaking her head. Gone. Just like that.

After we stubbed our cigarettes, I reached across the table and brushed my thumb across the tan line where her wedding ring used to be. Our fingers interlocked, and I slid my chair closer to hers across the kitchen linoleum. We kissed very softly on the lips.

I haven't been with another man since I was a teenager, she said. I *feel* like a teenager.

Me too, I lied.

With our clothes off, we chose to make what we were doing count. There was no need to be bashful. She told me what she wanted, mouth here, hands there, and I did as she said. The erotic geometries aligned very nicely. Seen from above and behind, her body had the elegance of a double helix—arms thrust forward and crossed, back in the shape of an hourglass, her spine a dotted line. She wanted it rough and loud, as if to shatter all memory of her husband, so we wrestled with the ferocity of quarreling lovers overcoming the quarrel, then we rested and did it again, more tenderly this time.

We smoked a cigarette in bed, and the talk turned to our families, as I'd felt sure it would—her mother dead of cancer far too young, my brother dead of a bullet in the brain even younger. I didn't belabor the point, and neither did she. We mentioned these facts only briefly, in passing, as if the specifics weren't required because we both already knew them, had known them all along. She rose and straddled me. She seemed to know what I wanted without my even saying it. She wanted to taste me, she said, she wanted to taste herself on me, and I offered her everything.

Don't go, she said. Sleep here. Just a few hours. I have to be up for work at six. We can get coffee from the deli on the corner.

Once in the night she rolled over, and amid the gauzy confusion of half sleep I remembered I was lying next to a stranger, an attractive stranger, and I smelled her hair and the smell of sex. I moved on top of her, and she woke and moaned and arched her back.

At six her alarm went off. While she showered, I dressed and went for coffee. We shared a cigarette at the kitchen table, exhausted and guarded, unsure of how to say goodbye.

We kissed in her doorway, and she watched me leave, leaning out into the hallway just as she had when I'd arrived.

Outside, the predawn streets were nearly empty. The light was cold and lunar, the sky the color of a daguerreotype. I bought a newspaper for the subway ride home, but when the train came I couldn't read. I stared out the window at the darkness of the passing tunnel.

Each time I called the talk line, I hoped to hear Molly's voice; every time I was disappointed. I had her cell phone number, she had my home number, but neither of us made the move. Something about the way we'd met made a friendly call—unmediated by four menu prompts and the perky-bimbo voice—too intimate, too presumptuous.

One night I connected with a woman named Ashley seeking a horny young stud from my particular neighborhood. She was bossy, and her bossiness turned me on. She ordered me to take off my clothes, and I did. She ordered me to put on a pair of running shorts, and I did. She told me she wanted me to go to a certain street corner in Queens, pretend I'd been out for a run when I realized I'd locked myself out of my apartment, and ask her boyfriend, who would be waiting there smoking a cigarette, to use his telephone, and, once inside the boyfriend's apartment, first make a pretend call to a friend with a set of spare keys and then, profoundly grateful for the use of the telephone, submit to the boyfriend's wish to get down on his knees and go to work with his mouth. Then she repeated her instructions, beginning to end. I confessed I was only interested in meeting her. She said that would come later: first, the boyfriend. She wanted to hear all about my cock from her boyfriend. When I told her no, she became petulant, and I noticed a slight burr in her voice.

This ain't no boyfriend-girlfriend thing, I said. Your voice is too breathy, too nasal, like you're pretending to be someone you're not. You sound like—

He didn't let me say it. He pressed star and was gone.

One weekend afternoon a "cute little uptown Dominican, 36-C, all natural, no implants" sent a message. She said she needed to get off before she rehearsed that night with her rock band. We connected, exchanged vitals. I gave her directions to my place. It was all very straightforward, simple as summoning a plumber.

When she arrived, she said, Some guys think I look underage. I can show you ID if you want.

I didn't think she looked underage, nor did I want to card her as if she were buying cigarettes. Her hair was shoulder-length and shiny, like delicate strands of obsidian, and her skin smelled of lavender. She seemed incapable of looking me in the eye but made up for it by being very frank. I offered to make us tea, or a whiskey Coke, whatever she wanted, whatever would help her relax. She shrugged and looked at the floor. After a moment, she said, Why don't we just, like, fuck?

When we were through I offered her a cigarette. I lit one for myself and reclined on the bed next to her. She said, Most guys I've met only last, like, five minutes at the most.

They don't like to look at my face. They bend me over and do it and then they want me to leave.

I wanted her to leave but I knew it would be callous to say so.

I only lasted five minutes, I said.

Yeah, but at least you know something about foreplay.

How many guys have you met off the line?

Oh, I don't know. Maybe, like, a dozen. Maybe more. Why?

Why do I do it?

Yeah.

I don't know. I suppose I shouldn't.

She was quiet for a moment.

It's just that nothing's, like, permanent. So why not admit it and stop trying to find someone to be with forever? I guess my dad's death made me realize everything can be gone tomorrow. Might as well enjoy today.

Her voice became inflectionless, deadly matter-of-fact.

He was hit by a drunk driver when I was six. Right down the street from our house, right in the middle of the day. When I heard the sirens I came out of the house. There was blood, like, everywhere. I saw a body in the street. The head was barely attached. The cops told me to go home. In a little while they came to the door and told us it was my dad. I didn't even recognize him when I saw him in the street.

I told her about my brother killing himself with a semi-automatic assault rifle, about how I'd gone to the police and had them make copies of the crime scene photos for me, the gun and the body and the blood on the walls. This seemed to make her feel better.

Before she left, she said, You know, I never do this twice with the same guy.

That's okay, I said.

But take care and good luck and stuff.

You too, I said.

For days afterward, the words of the cute Dominican girl resounded in my mind, a prod to my imagination. *Body, blood, head barely attached . . .* I could only escape them by stepping into the streets and walking for hours through the vastness of Queens, past the all-night bodegas and the empty factories, the ill-lit rail yards and the derelict water-fronts. I dressed in a suit and tie, a flaneur of the city's dark edges—inviting curious glances and the possibility of violence—and I often ended the evening by climbing the fire escape of an old factory in Long Island City, watching from the roof as the elevated trains crawled below me like silver caterpillars. I smoked and tossed my cigarettes onto North-ern Boulevard, seven stories below, where they exploded in a flower of sparks. I thought of the tower jumpers, twirling in the air like my cigarette, their quick and poignant plunge to the pavement, their escape from life an escape from pain.

Now when I wrote for the paper the stakes felt higher, and with Seidel as my example—the writer willing to say the unsayable in a climate of fear and self-censorship, flinging daggers that sang toward the unsuspecting reader—I chose my subjects with greater care. Still, it was easier as a journalist. I could simply quote the words of others, neither condemning nor condoning. In a profile of jazz trumpeter Dave Douglas, for instance, I quoted him calling the war in Afghanistan "more of a trade show and a laboratory for new weapons than a real pursuit of those who perpetrated that horrible event" already known by the glib shorthand 9/11. Indeed. It would take a decade for the mastermind to be snuffed, and the country where the plan was hatched would remain a failed state and a cesspool of extremism despite the best efforts of our misused soldiers, but it wasn't as if the paper's subscribers were looking to the arts pages for an understanding of the "war on terror."

The assignment I enjoyed most occurred when Ray asked me to write a profile of a radical performance artist named William Pope.L. He'd once walked the streets of New York with a twelve-foot white phallus strapped to his midsection, a comment on white fears of black sexuality that sent the National Endowment for the Arts—which had once bestowed on Pope.L a grant of taxpayer money—into a tizzy. His most famous work, however, involved eating a copy of the *Wall Street Journal* with the aid of ketchup and milk, then regurgitating the meal, all while sitting on a gleaming porcelain toilet perched atop a ten-foot scaffold. He told me he'd once seen an ad campaign for the paper that made it out to be the modern equivalent of a primitive cultural object imbued with mystical powers. I quoted his explanation at length:

"The ads suggested that if you bought a subscription, good things would happen to you. They proposed that the paper could have a magical effect. You didn't have to read it. Just having it near you, having it land on your doorstep, would multiply your wealth."

It was Ray's brilliant idea to hold the piece until the day the paper, after more than a century in existence, first enlivened its pages with color ink. Thus I could quip that we'd spiced up the product mainly for the sake of its digestibility, an ironic bit of institutional self-mockery that, far from buttressing Pope.L's critique, laughed and winked at it. Nothing I wrote elicited more comments from my colleagues, and everyone thought it was a gas. With each compliment I grew more uneasy, until I began to understand that my habit of privately laughing and winking at myself, at least in relation to my work—the self-proclaimed democratic socialist, working as a low-level functionary at a rag whose very name was practically synonymous with the triumph of finance capitalism—had now spilled over into my writing about others. I had come, at last, to inhabit the voice of a trapped man who perversely enjoyed his cage.

I was running out of tricks on the talk line. My clever come-ons had begun to bore even me, and I heard the same voices time and again, reciting their own rote greetings: Brown Sugar, Mistress Tina, dozens of others who never gave their names but whose intonations were as familiar as old friends. What had once surprised me—the novelty

of amateur pleasure seekers finding a voice for their fantasies, seeking a sympathetic listener to enliven and validate
them—now struck me as not much more than a lurid form
of group therapy in which true self-awareness remained forever elusive. Like all good things, the sounds of a working
vibrator or the click of a pair of handcuffs became first dull
and eventually repulsive with ceaseless repetition.

One night Molly called me at home. She said she'd been
out with a friend, having a drink, and she'd told the friend our
story—our improbable, slightly kinky, strangely sweet story.

I think of you a lot, out there in the city, she said. I wonder sometimes what you're doing.

I think about you too, I said.

An hour later I was at her door.

We sat at the table, just like the first time. We drank
a beer and smoked a cigarette, just like the first time. We
talked about little things, work and such. Then she told me
how, on a recent trip home, she'd found some cassette tapes
her mother had stowed in the attic. Her mother had made
them not long before her death, conversations with a psychic
in which the psychic had made a cryptic reference to a lover.
Molly's mother confirmed that there was "someone special"
in her life.

After listening to the tapes, Molly asked her mother's
best friend about this mention of a lover. The friend said
that Molly's mother had indeed had a lover, outside of her
marriage, for forty years.

Was he my real dad? Molly asked. She wondered because
she didn't look anything like her father. Many times her

mother had hinted that Molly was special, somehow different than her siblings.

Yes, the friend said, the lover was your father. He was also, she said, my son.

Molly was stunned. All these years the woman she'd known as her mother's best friend had been her grandmother too.

Life just gets more complicated, she said. One day you're walking along, deep in your routine, you've got a husband you love and a father you have no reason to think is not your father, and the next day you've got neither, but also somehow more. Everything you ever assumed is turned upside down.

We went to the bedroom and undressed. It felt very uncomplicated. This gesture has this effect. This movement elicits this response. This part fits here.

Silently we joined, as if picking the lock on a door to forgetfulness.

For a long time I didn't mention my phone-sex forays to anyone. Then an old friend from college, Rebecca, invited me to Arizona for a week of work and solitude at a little cabin she'd rented for the winter. We wrote in the mornings—she was at work on a novel—read and walked in the afternoons, made dinner together in the evenings. We talked about politics, books, and personal matters; there were few people in the world I was happier to listen to, and none I knew who listened more intently. One night over dinner and a bottle of wine I told her about my calls to the talk line, my meetings with Molly. If anyone would get it, then Rebecca surely would. It wasn't in her nature to be prudish or judgmental. She was the coolest cookie I'd ever known, as shrewd and nonchalant as a cat.

Little did I know just how well she'd understand, for when I finished she surprised me with a story of her own.

She was on her way out of the house, and the phone rang. It was a man. He spoke haltingly at first. She could barely make him out. Eventually she understood he was a graduate student at the University of Michigan. For a seminar in human sexuality, he was conducting random telephone surveys. He wondered if she could spare a moment to answer a few questions.

She told him she was already running late. She had to give a lecture in half an hour. She was sorry but she didn't have time.

Can I call back later? he asked.

Yes, I suppose, she said, although there was an edge of desperation in his voice that almost made her say no.

What is your lecture about? he asked.

She told him. She was an expert in her area of interest, and he was impressed.

Tell me one other thing before I go, he said.

What's that? she said.

Tell me what you're wearing to the lecture.

She was surprised by the question, but she looked at herself in the mirror.

I'm wearing a peach-colored dress, she said.

A woman in a peach dress on a spring day. That's nice.

The way he said those words—*a woman in a peach dress on a spring day*—both excited and frightened her.

I have to go, she said.

Okay. I'll call back later, he said.

She gave her lecture. Afterward, people asked her questions for an hour, and she came home exhausted and exhilarated. She made herself some dinner.

The telephone rang. It was the man again. He said his name was Joseph. He had just a few questions. It wouldn't take long.

But first, how was your lecture? he asked.

She told him about it, told him it had gone well, and he said, with what seemed to her sincerity, that he was happy to hear it. She felt a sudden flush in her face, a little surge of self-satisfaction. It had been a long time since she'd heard warm affirmation in a male voice.

He said he was going to ask her a series of questions about her sex life. When she heard the phrase, she laughed.

Why do you laugh? he asked.

Because I don't have a sex life, she said. My husband left me. I found out he was sleeping with his secretary. Maybe I should give you *his* number.

She laughed bitterly.

I'm sorry, he said. That's awful.

It's okay, she said. I'm glad he's gone. In some ways it's the most terrible thing that's ever happened to me, but in others it's been a blessing. I'm learning things about myself I wouldn't have otherwise. I can eat cereal for dinner if I don't feel like cooking. I've started mountaineering and I've lost forty pounds. I feel better inside my own skin than I ever have.

He asked her several generic questions—her age now, at what age she'd had her first sexual experience, how many partners she'd been with, whether she'd ever had an abortion or a sexually transmitted disease, how many times per week, on average, she'd had sex with her husband. She answered them all.

His questions became more intimate. He asked her whether she liked to perform oral sex, whether she liked to receive oral sex, whether she'd ever had anal sex, whether she'd ever had lesbian fantasies, lesbian experiences. She began to feel uncomfortable but she answered his questions. He sounded a little embarrassed to be asking them. When he was done, he thanked her, and they said goodbye.

A few days later he called back.

I tried to reach you a couple of times, he said. But I only got your answering machine. Rebecca. I like that name. And I missed your voice. I wanted to hear it again.

She was flattered—and apprehensive. She'd made a point of not telling him her name when he called before. She hadn't thought he'd call again. But she talked to him. She liked the sound of his voice too, although she didn't tell him that.

He began to call every few days. She looked forward to hearing from him. It was a pleasant distraction from her work, from her loneliness in the house she'd once shared with her husband. He was a good listener, and she did most of the talking—about work, about the new life she'd suddenly found herself living.

One day he asked again what she was wearing. She told him. What are you wearing underneath? he asked. She was surprised by the question—surprised and a little turned on.

Will you take it off? he asked. All of it?

Yes, she said. If you want me to.

He continued to call. Each time, they had phone sex—he would talk, she would touch herself. He said that he loved to give her pleasure; it made him feel good to make her feel good. She enjoyed it too. She'd ceased to have any interest in sex when her husband left, so disgusted was she by his philandering. Joseph was helping her discover a portion of herself she thought had vanished for good. His voice soothed her. She got lost inside of it as she touched herself.

She sometimes worried, though, that he was in cahoots with people who wanted to tarnish her reputation. She worried that he was taping their calls. She often worked with people who fought corruption in large corporations, and her work had cost those corporations serious money. Corporate lawyers and operatives had searched high and low for ways to discredit her, to no avail. She wondered if they might be getting desperate.

It was too late now. She could only hope that he was telling the truth.

One day he called and said, I have to confess, I lied to you.

Her throat tightened, her hands began to shake.

I wasn't doing a survey, he said, although I did call your number at random. I'd just received some terrible news, and I was lonely. I didn't have anyone to talk to. I just started dialing numbers, and you were the first person who answered. So I made up a reason to talk to you.

What's wrong? she asked. What happened?

I don't really want to tell you, he said. It's my problem. I don't want to drag that into what we have.

So you're not a student, she said.

No. I'm a landscape architect. I don't live in Michigan. I live in Chicago. But I did go to college in Michigan about fifteen years ago.

He told her about his work, how much he loved it—being outdoors and doing creative things and making the world a tiny bit more beautiful. Moved by his passion, she forgave his lie, although she wondered why he couldn't tell her what had happened to him.

The next time he called, she said, Guess what? I'm coming to Chicago to give a talk. I'd like to meet you. But I understand if you'd rather not.

No, he said. I'd like that too. More than I can tell you.

They arranged to meet in the lobby of a hotel.

A part of her knew she shouldn't do it. He'd lied to her at least once. He could be a sociopath, a serial seducer of vulnerable women. She told no one where she was going. How could she? As she drove to the hotel, she became very afraid. She might disappear, might end up at the bottom of a river somewhere, dumped in a landfill, any number of horrible places, and no one would know how or why. She hadn't left word with a soul. But she went ahead. She was too curious to turn back.

He was waiting in the lobby.

He was tall, sandy-haired, lean and tan from working outdoors. He wore elegant, thin-framed glasses. She thought him quite handsome. His face exuded a thoughtful calm. When he spotted her looking at him, he smiled.

They went up to his room.

As soon as they entered the room, they undressed. They made love, rested, talked, made love, rested, talked—all day long and into the night.

Once, when she came back from the bathroom, he was doubled over on the bed, holding his stomach.

Are you okay? she asked.

Yes, I'm fine, he said. Just a little indigestion.

They slept. In the morning, they showered, dressed, and checked out. He walked her to her car.

Thank you, he said. You have no idea how great a gift you've given me.

When my husband left, I was sure I'd never make love to anyone again, she said. What we've had—what we have— is so precious.

They hugged, and she drove away, feeling both invigorated and a little apart from herself, as if she'd been watching herself in a movie.

A few days later, he called.

Listen, I have to tell you the truth now, he said.

Here it comes, she thought. *My whole life is about to unravel.*

In the hotel room, when you asked me if I was okay—well, I'm not okay. That first day I called you, I'd just been diagnosed with pancreatic cancer. I was told I probably had less than a year to live.

She tried to speak, but nothing came out of her mouth. She did the math in her head—it had been five months since that first call.

He told her he was married. When he got the news about the cancer, he drove alone in his car for hours. He couldn't bring himself to go home and tell his wife. He'd hidden his doctor visits from her, hoping it was nothing serious, not wanting to alarm her. Suddenly their days together were numbered. Her life was about to be torn apart, and she didn't even know it. His was about to be over. He thought about ways of killing himself, speeding up the inevitable: driving his car into a tree, jumping off a bridge. That's when he started dialing random numbers, unable to bear his solitude, and when he heard her voice he composed himself and made up a story, because she sounded kind, and he didn't want to scare her, he wanted to talk to her—he wanted, somehow, to connect.

Oh, Joseph, you should have told me.

No. Then it wouldn't have been the same. None of this would have happened. The whole thing would have been colored by sadness. I'm a married man. You would have pitied me, or been disgusted by me. You've allowed me to have something apart from all that, to create something new, one final thing. I couldn't have lasted this long without you. But I want you to know I don't have much time now. I might not be calling as often.

Just call when you can, she said. Please. Call my cell phone if you don't reach me at home. Please.

She gave him her cell phone number.

When he called, they no longer had phone sex. They talked about his illness, about his preparations for death, and when he got tired of talking about that, they talked about her work.

One day he called, but she didn't recognize his voice at first. He was very weak. It was just before Thanksgiving. He strained to tell her that he didn't have the energy to speak very much, but could she please tell him what she was doing for Thanksgiving, whether she would see her family, anything at all about her plans. His life, he said, was over now. He was simply waiting to die. He envied people with plans other than dying.

She broke down and cried, trembled uncontrollably with helplessness. Then, when the sobs had run their course, she got ahold of herself, for his sake. She blew her nose and wiped her eyes. She told him she would visit her parents in the little town where they lived. She would help them cook dinner for the whole family, all the children and grandchildren, the first great-grandchild of her still-living grandmother, and she told him everything they would make, all their favorite Thanksgiving food, turkey, gravy, mashed potatoes, creamed green beans, rolls and marmalade, pecan pie.

I wish I could eat, he said. I miss having an appetite.

Those were the last words she remembered him saying. He had whispered them. She'd barely been able to hear him.

They never spoke again.

A few weeks later, her phone rang. It was a woman. My name is Elan, she said. I don't know you, but I'm Joseph's sister. He asked me to call you and thank you for your friendship. He passed away quietly last week, in the company of family. He wanted you to know.

When Rebecca finished her story, I was shattered. It was so improbable, so heartbreaking—a strange act of connection amid the horror of impending death. We talked for a while about the mysteries of chance, about the link between mortality and desire, and then I went to my room in the cottage. Without thinking, I picked up the phone. When I reached for the keypad, poised to dial with my index finger, I realized I had no idea whom I'd meant to call. I suppose it was a reflex, triggered by empathy for Joseph and Rebecca both. I couldn't articulate it at the time, but I must have begun to understand that phone sex had kept alive a part of myself I feared losing, just as it had for Rebecca, and that the solace of strangers on a telephone was the only solace that seemed attainable, just as it had for Joseph. Their story, adjusting for the particulars, had a spooky resonance with my own.

For a second I played one of those mental games that seem so absurd in retrospect. Do I replace the receiver in the cradle and admit I experienced a flickering instance of dementia, the body acting without direction or consent from the mind? Or do I recover myself, think of a number to dial, and trick myself into believing I'd had a purpose in picking up the phone all along? I opted for a harmless bit of self-deception and called my home number, thinking I ought to check for messages left in my absence. There was only one. It was, of all people, Molly.

When I returned to New York, I called her. This time, I said, I want to take you out on an honest-to-god date. Let's meet for a drink.

I told her the address of a bar I liked.

She was waiting at a table, sipping a beer, when I arrived. She told me her work was going well. She was part of a group show at a gallery, and people were impressed by her photos. She also had a new job assisting an artist, a well-known painter, and she enjoyed it. She answered his mail, ran his errands, traveled with him to Mexico City when a show of his work opened there. He had friends in the movie and the music industries, and she was meeting a lot of talented people. She'd even started dating someone—tentatively, but it was going well. No rush, nothing serious, just enjoying each other's company. She and her husband were about to finalize their divorce.

We had several drinks, moved into the same side of the booth, held hands. It felt very sweet, almost innocent, a strange turn given how we'd met, what we'd made of the meeting. At the sound of the bartender counting the change in his till, we looked around and discovered we were the last two people in the place.

We hailed a taxi and took it to her apartment. I walked her to the door.

I have to be to work pretty early, she said. I should get a good night's rest.

Me too, I said. I'm glad we did this.

I gave her a hug. We kissed on the lips, briefly, lightly, and then she turned and was gone.

I decided to walk home, across the width of Manhattan and over the Fifty-ninth Street Bridge, past the riverside projects and up through Long Island City to its border with Astoria. The night was beautiful, clear and crisp. It was a Sunday. The city was quiet. Partway across the bridge, I looked back at the skyline, that proud, almost disdainful skyline, still proud despite its diminishment. Standing there, suspended above the shining black surface of the East River, I had a hunch I'd never see her again, that she'd disappeared forever among that glittering immensity of glass and steel. We'd done everything backward, and now, still moving backward, it was as if we were entering the time before our first date, before I'd ever known her.

Not long afterward, I gave up calling the talk line. At the time I suppose I'd have said I quit because I grew bored with the predictability of it, and because from a cost-benefit point of view it was nuts. But it may not have been entirely coincidental that around this time I finally realized there could be no substitute for the missed connection about which I fantasized most. All through my foray into phone sex I kept opening that envelope of photographs taken by the police when they'd discovered my brother's body, and each and every time I imagined the call I should have placed to him on the day he died, the consoling words I might have offered, the gesture of brotherly love he might have accepted as a reason to go on living another day. Equally likely, I belatedly realized, was the possibility that nothing could have dissuaded him, that my call would have been in vain, and whatever I said or did not say would have become the source of my regret, instead of my failure to call at all.

Among the remnants of his life I'd tracked down, in addition to the official reports, was his final phone bill from US West Communications, a piece of paper I often studied for hints about his state of mind at the end. The time span of the phone bill made its meager data particularly stark, even if they only served to multiply the uncertainties.

The bill claimed to cover activity through July 1, 1996, though it was dated June 12. It showed he was due a refund of $11.96. He paid for some services a month in advance, and the previous bill ran through June 1. This final bill, then, contained information, spookily enough, for just one day—the last day of his life, June 2, 1996. It listed three long-distance calls, all to Minnesota, one to our parents in Tracy, the others to our sister in Granite Falls. He placed the first at 11:04 a.m. The call lasted four minutes. Our mother and father had returned home from church and were in the midst of making lunch. It was 12:04 p.m. their time. They said they'd call him back when they finished eating and they did as promised.

June 2, 11:04 a.m., Mountain Standard Time: the first of his three long-distance calls. Had he called to say goodbye without coming straight out with the word goodbye? My mother recalled telling him that perhaps if he gave Wendy some time to think things over, they might still work it out.

Oh, I'm going to give her a lot of time to think, she remembered him saying.

Was there a clue in those words? A note of warning?

My sister received the other two long-distance calls he made that day, though she had no reason to suspect he called twice, since she wasn't home for either call and he only left one message. He placed the first call shortly after he finished speaking with our parents, at 12:16 p.m. his time, the second at 1:52 p.m., each call lasting less than a minute. When Lisa arrived home to find his message she was surprised. In the two years since she'd left home and moved in with her boyfriend, Dan had not called her once. His voice mail was so out of character that it gave her cause to worry. For him to have called, she thought, something must be up. Something must be wrong. She immediately picked up the phone and dialed his number. He did not answer. She left him a message. He did not return the call.

What changed for him between the time he left a message and the time she left one back? Why did he try not once but twice to call her—a thing, it bears repeating, he'd never done before that day—and then not a third time when he knew the call would be answered? In her message she'd made sure to say she'd be home the rest of the day. If he'd tried a third time he'd have reached her. Did he go from desperately seeking a lifeline to abandoning all hope for a lifeline in the span of a few hours? Was it the afternoon of drinking with friends that changed something? Was it the evening conversation with Wendy that crystallized his fate?

The phone bill listed one further piece of pertinent data. It showed that at 9:15 p.m. he dialed *69 to activate last-call return, for which he was charged seventy-five cents. What could it mean? Someone had called him while he was otherwise occupied, and he hadn't answered in time? Someone had called him and failed to leave a message, his answering machine recording nothing but the sound of the hang-up, and he wanted to know who it was? Or he'd been away from his apartment for a time, returned with a hope that someone had called, perhaps Wendy, and finding no message on his machine he checked for a missed call anyway?

Ultimately, all this piece of paper told me, despite my hopes for more, was that he was still alive at 9:15 p.m. on the night he did himself in. That left a six-hour window between my mother telling me to call him and his last known effort to reach for something outside of himself, six hours the better part of which I'd spent in bed with Marie. In my most self-lacerating moods I imagined our bodies joined in pleasure as, two thousand miles away, he leaned into the barrel of the gun.

Once the arts and editorial pages were settled again in Manhattan, in temporary quarters above the West Side Garment District, the men in the suites looked again for places to squeeze. Eventually a quarter of the company's workforce would be cut, and Ray Sokolov was among those to leave. At the age of sixty, after twenty years of service to the company, he was enticed to take early retirement and replaced by a genial reactionary who'd cut his teeth at the Moonie-owned *Washington Times*. I was unsurprised when, shortly thereafter, word came down that the Leisure & Arts page would more fully integrate its coverage with the editorial page, whose mantra, "free markets and free people," unwittingly tipped its hand by which of the two it placed first.

Soon it came to pass that I was given a chance to work on pieces of greater world-political import. I was sitting with my feet on my desk, editing a story about a play in Chicago or the lovely wines of the Alsace, when Paul Gigot asked me to follow him into an empty conference room. He invited me to sit. He cut straight to the chase. He said that for the foreseeable future I would continue copyediting for the Leisure & Arts page, but beginning in a few weeks I would do the same for the editorial page of the *Wall Street Journal's* European edition.

I told him I didn't want to do that.

He seemed surprised.

I told him I didn't agree with the politics of the page— with its viewpoint on just about everything.

He said he wasn't asking me to write things I didn't believe. He was asking me to edit copy for spelling, punctuation, and grammar.

I told him I didn't want my hands on the editorial page in any way, shape, or form.

He said he would give me a small raise in compensation for my added responsibilities, and I would do whatever he told me to do.

I thanked him for the raise.

A college friend of mine, M.J., wrote that spring and told me she'd secured a gig as a fire lookout in southern New Mexico. She suggested I lift my flabby keister out of my cubicle and come have a look at the country, breathe some clean air, unplug for a moment from the rat race. In late May I booked another flight to Albuquerque, where I planned to rummage around for a couple days in my brother's past before heading south for a rendezvous with M.J., a trip on which I would blow my yearly paid vacation and, with luck, find the answer to the question of what I should be next.

Almost in spite of myself, in spite of my calculated evasion of the title in my so-called career, I was still for a little while longer a reporter, though one without pretense to worldly concerns, much less objectivity or evenhandedness. I made a date to visit the family who'd known Dan best at the end, thinking they of all people might know something I didn't: his boss George, George's wife Barbara, and their daughter Emily, all of whom I'd met on my first visit to New Mexico, when Emily and Dan were still engaged. I hadn't talked to them since the last time I saw Dan alive. I'd met them only that once. For reasons of distance and logistics, I didn't make it to Dan's memorial service in Albuquerque, and they didn't attend the funeral in Minnesota. It was hard to avoid the feeling that we were strangers communing over the memory of a ghost—a ghost who, seven and a half years earlier, had sat with us one evening after dinner and taken our phony money in a game of Monopoly, laughing as he filled the board with hotels, confident and happy and secure in the love of what he thought were his future in-laws.

Emily and Barbara were at the kitchen table looking through boxes of pictures when I arrived. They wanted to give me some snapshots of Dan. Barbara offered me a beer. Emily talked of her family; less than a year after she'd ended things with Dan, and not long before his death, she'd married someone else and now had two little children. She'd also found God, and this had led her to the belief that everything had worked out according to plan, that the Lord Jesus had known Dan was in trouble, and had sent her a signal to bail before she got caught up in trouble she couldn't escape.

Our conversation danced around the edge of the reason I'd come there. No one knew how to talk about him for more than a minute or two. I wasn't surprised; I could count on one hand the number of times I'd found someone willing to talk about him for longer than a minute or two in the six years since his death.

George said, Come here, I want to show you something.

He led me to the dining room. Against one wall stood a china cabinet Dan had made for him, an elegant piece fashioned from oak, with natural stain and a lustrous wax finish. I'd seen similar pieces in other homes, always beautiful and perfectly functional, including in the home of my parents, but no matter how many times I looked at his work it always impressed me with its craftsmanship.

The kid was good, George said. He took care. Not just with woodwork, but everything he did.

Emily took us to the guest bedroom and pointed to another of his pieces, a chest of drawers.

Dan made that for me when we first started dating, she said. I think he even signed it on the back of the bottom drawer.

Sure enough, when we pulled it out we found the words, *To Emily, From Dan, With Love.* We all stood in awkward silence. I turned away from the sight of a tear tracing the curve of Emily's cheek.

George and I went together to the back yard, where more of Dan's handiwork awaited: the swimming pool he'd helped George build, the shed they'd put up in which to store Dan's hot air balloon. George spoke of summer afternoons they'd spent together grilling food, swimming in the pool, drinking beer, telling stories.

Even after Dan and Emily broke up, George said, we remained friends. It wasn't easy for Emily. It was pretty awkward, if you want to know the truth. She thought of it as taking sides, but I couldn't cut him out of my life.

George admitted—quietly, seemingly out of the side of his mouth—that he'd sought counseling after Dan's death. He alone bore the horror of having discovered Dan's body.

I wouldn't have known this if I hadn't chased down the police report. But it was right there on the last page:

> Ofc. Faerber advised that the decedent was found by a co-worker named George Goodwin. Mr. Goodwin had gone to the apartment to check on the welfare of the decedent because he had failed to show for work. Mr. Goodwin was able to gain access via the pass key provided by the building manager. Ofc. Faerber further advised that Mr. Goodwin had become startled upon discovery of the decedent. Mr. Goodwin then accidentally broke the stair rail from the wall. Mr. Goodwin did not proceed any further than the top of the stairs of the apartment interior. . . .

George led me back inside, where he retired to his study for the evening. The memories, it seemed, were too painful to explore any further.

One of the things I wanted to know was what had happened the morning his body was discovered. Six years had passed since that day, but I knew less than I thought I should about the hours surrounding the gunshot. I still believed that if I could tease a comprehensive narrative from those hours, I might be freed at last from the grip of a morbid devotion to the mystery of his death. Now that George was gone, I delicately broached the subject with Barbara. Between what she told me and what I'd read in the police report, the basic story of that morning came into as sharp a focus as it ever would.

It wasn't like Dan to be late for work. George tried to call around ten o'clock. He hoped Dan had had too much to drink, was sleeping off a hangover. The phone rang. No answer until the machine picked up. George left a message. He tried to make a joke of it but he couldn't hide the worry in his voice.

He left the work site where his crew was installing fiber-optic cable, the crew on which Dan was foreman. On his way home he drove past Dan's apartment. Dan's truck was parked in front of his door. George circled through the parking lot and left without stopping.

When George got home he told his wife that Dan was AWOL.

Why don't you go check on him? Barbara asked.

I went by, he said. His truck's still there.

He paused.

I don't know. I've got a bad feeling.

What do you mean, a bad feeling?

He's never been late. Something must be wrong.

Did you knock on his door?

No, George said.

He's probably hungover and sleeping in.

Yeah, George said. I suppose you're right.

He dialed Dan's number again. This time he didn't leave a message.

Just drive over and wake him up, Barbara said.

George loitered around the house. Twenty minutes passed.

Do you want me to go with you? Barbara said.

No, that's all right, George said. I'll do it.

He got in his truck. He drove to the apartment and parked in the lot. He waited for several minutes, unsure of what to do. If he hadn't known Dan so well he might have been less concerned, but the kid was more to him than a hired hand. In the year since his daughter had broken off her engagement to Dan, George had walked a tightrope, honoring Emily's decision but maintaining his closeness with the young man who was to have been his son-in-law. He worked with him every day. He still respected him. It had been difficult, no doubt about it. His jumbled-up feelings of loyalty to both of them. His hopes for both of them.

Now he sat paralyzed with dread.

He thought about driving off, just leaving, waiting at the work site until Dan showed. Finally, though, he worked up the courage to get out of his truck and go to the door.

He knocked. No answer. He knocked again. No sound of anyone stirring. He tried the door. It was locked.

He went to the office and found the manager, a guy by the name of Jones. He explained the situation. Jones got his keys. Another employee named Roschevitz joined them. They walked together to No. E43. Jones gave George the key.

George slipped the key in the lock. The door gave way. Inside, the shades were drawn, the apartment mostly dark, just one lamp on. He saw a figure sitting on the couch. He called Dan's name, but there was no answer.

He started into the apartment. He made it a few feet. Then he saw the wound in the side of Dan's head. He became very afraid. He tried to turn and leave, but in turning he pulled too hard on the handrail along the entryway steps. It gave way, tore from the wall. George stumbled on the stairs, righted himself, got himself out of the apartment. Jones looked at him and said, What is it?

The cops, George said, call the cops.

At the kitchen table, Emily and Barbara told more stories. Emily said that toward the end of her relationship with Dan, he'd been drinking a lot.

It was like there were two sides to him, she said. He was different when he drank. He got angry. One night he threw a glass against the wall and it shattered everywhere. That's when I started having second thoughts about marriage. I wondered if I really knew him. I couldn't figure out the source of his anger.

Barbara said that on the day before Dan killed himself he'd brought his gun to their house and sat at the kitchen table, exactly where we were now, and spent an hour or more cleaning it. This was the day after Wendy—the new woman, the one he'd started seeing after Emily called off the wedding—had broken up with him. Barbara's mother, who'd been visiting that same day, later said she had an inkling Dan was suicidal, something in his voice and in his eyes, a hint of despair, the tenderness he'd shown the gun, as if preparing it for a moment of truth. She later wished

she'd done something for him, something that would have
saved him.

In this she was not alone.

Emily asked, Did your parents hate me when I called off
the wedding? Were they angry with me? Did they blame me
for what happened?

I assured her they did not.

Barbara left the table, and Emily and I sat there alone.
She talked about traveling to Minnesota to meet my family
for the first time, not long after she and Dan confirmed their
engagement.

I felt like a queen, she said.

Everywhere they went people were thrilled to see Dan
again, and all were curious about his bride-to-be. The enthusiasm with which they were greeted almost made her want
to move to Minnesota. Some of Dan's antics gave her pause,
though, such as the midnight run of sign-stealing he and a
friend had made on the lesser-traveled country roads, the
sort of thing he and his buddies had done in high school and
apparently had yet to grow out of. Emily, still a teenager
herself, not even out of high school, didn't exactly find her
fiancé's behavior indicative of maturity.

She leaned across the table, and a hush came over her
voice.

I don't know why, she half whispered, but I feel a strong
connection to you. Like you're my brother in a weird way.
I know that makes no sense, since we only saw each other
once before, but maybe we went through some of the same
things afterward.

Yes, I told her, no doubt we did.

There's something I want to ask you, she said. Dan had a secret. I'm pretty sure I'm the only person he ever told, but I wonder if he told you too.

I wasn't sure what she meant but I couldn't think of any secret.

I don't know if I should share it now, she said. I mean, if you agree to keep someone's secret do you still have to keep it after he's gone?

I didn't want to encourage the notion that she ought to keep his secret but I suspected she required a nuanced response if she was going to give it up. So I improvised.

I told her that my situation was unique: if I didn't destroy all my notebooks, people would learn certain things about me after my death that might surprise them, and I had come to accept this. I couldn't presume to tell her what to do, but I made clear I was curious about anything that could help me better understand my brother, especially since I could no longer ask him directly.

Just then Barbara walked back in the room.

You know, it's getting late, Emily said. I need to get the kids to bed. I should show Phil how to get to his hotel. He can follow me there. I'll see you guys tomorrow.

I hugged Barbara and said good night and wished her well, promised to keep in touch.

Emily and I drove to the hotel separately. We stood in the parking lot, in the warm night air of the desert, making more small talk. At last she dropped her bombshell.

What she wanted to tell me was that my brother had

been raped. Dan had shared this with her not long before they broke up, when he knew he was losing her and was drinking hard in an effort to deny it. He'd been just a child when it happened, seven or eight years old, if she remembered correctly. When she told me Dan's description of the person who'd done it—a certain someone with an identifying characteristic "who Dan said you both hated when you were young"—I knew exactly whom he'd meant.

I couldn't bear to sit still with this news roaring inside my cranium, so I canceled my hotel reservation and drove south into the desert, windows rolled down, Satch and Duke's *The Great Summit* on the stereo, as loud as I could stand it. I tried to hold my concentration to the lines on the road even as I felt something cold and hard calve inside of me like a glacier. Only past midnight did I finally fall asleep in the back seat of my rental car, alongside a lonely country road near Truth or Consequences, a place name whose bitter irony shadowed my feverish dreams. I had uncovered at last a hidden truth, though the consequences eluded me.

Into the Wilderness

Of all the friends I had in the world, M.J. was foremost among those whose company I could tolerate under the circumstances. Temperamentally, we could hardly have been more different. She rolled through the world freestyle, exuding irreverence and mirth, always leading with the heart. Though she'd known darkness, she'd chosen not to hunker down and live inside of it, but its traces could be seen if you looked hard enough, etched in subtle lines on her face. Once she left her little hometown in Nebraska she committed herself to a cosmopolitan life of adventure and travel and refused to look back. She'd spent time in Alaska, Ghana, the Sahara, Costa Rica; she was taking a summer of paid R&R stateside, in her fire tower, before she began a master's program in Argentina. She evinced a charming lack of guile that disguised a canny mind and allowed her to fit in anywhere, from the streets of Cairo to the cowboy bars of southern New Mexico. She stood five-foot-two and weighed a hundred pounds fully clothed; she chewed Levi Garrett and took her whiskey neat. To a guy like me she easily could have appeared a little too carefree: an impish world traveler in pigtails, a hell of a lot smarter than she let on, and more ambitious than she gave reason to suspect—a chameleon of sorts. Instead she'd drawn me, also a chameleon, irresistibly into her orbit, shown me things about openhearted friendship that I'd not known previously.

Her first offer to hang out had involved sneaking onto the University of Montana golf course at daybreak and sprinting through a round of speed golf before the clubhouse opened and the groundskeepers nabbed us for failing to pay greens fees. Her dedication to frivolity in all its forms was contagious. Telling her no just wasn't an option. We'd kept in touch for years by letter, and she never failed to entertain with comic stories from her travels. Hers was just the face—freckled, smiling, blue eyes twinkling with mischief—I needed to see, and there she was, standing outside the Hilltop Café in T or C, New Mexico, suntanned and lean as a mountain lion from hikes to and from her lookout all summer. Also, charmingly, still a little buzzed from a night spent at Elephant Butte Lake with some rowdy, off-duty firefighters.

We stopped for groceries before we left town, then I followed her by car across the creosote flats toward the rim of the Black Range. We drove through two little foothills villages, relics of the mining boom of the 1870s, into piñon-juniper country, then up into the taller, statelier ponderosa forest with its shaggy-needled, red-barked trees, the road all the while making serpentine curves. At a pass high on the divide we turned onto a dead-end dirt road, where we parked and began a two-hour hoof to her mountain with our packs.

It was strange country, foreign to my experience, the driest time of a dry season in the driest forest I'd ever known. The grasses were sere and brittle, wildflowers few. The needles of the pines crunched underfoot. In the beginning of the walk, at a little over eight thousand feet above sea level on a south-facing slope, we passed a few alligator junipers, as well as scattered oaks of various types and the occasional yucca in bloom. Higher up the ponderosas predominated, their faint scent of vanilla sweetening the air, and then we'd round a ridge and enter the mixed conifer of the cooler north slopes, dense and dark and fragrant with resins, the bark of the trees draped in lichens. For the last mile I labored, short of breath from cigarettes and sea-level living, until we topped out in an open meadow above ten thousand feet, where a tower rose another fifty feet in the air.

We dumped our packs against the concrete footers and climbed the sixty-five steps through a staggered series of four landings, each offering a more impressive tease than the last of what awaited on top. The view from the little glass-walled room nearly made me topple from vertigo. The Black Range ran north and south, scored by deep canyons on its east side, the most rugged country I had ever seen. The crest of the divide loomed like a bulwark blocking the view to the northwest, but in every other direction the vistas stretched for sixty, eighty, a hundred miles or more—long, open expanses of desert with scattered ramparts of rock beneath sky-island peaks. I gripped the windowsill and tried to take it all in as M.J. pointed out the distant landmarks, from the dark shoulder of the Manzanos just south of Albuquerque to the Tres Hermanas, three little pyramids marking the gateway to the Mexican border, peeking over the flinty shoulder of Cookes Peak—the Matterhorn of New Mexico, M.J. said, flashing air quotes with her fingers.

Not a bad view, huh? she said.

I've never seen anything like it. I think I'm already in love.

Crazy thing is you can watch all day, and it never looks the same for longer than an hour or two.

And they pay you for this.

I know. Can you believe it?

The next afternoon I walked. I felt myself drawn along the trails to the north and west, into the upper headwaters canyons of the Spirit Creek, where pink bluffs rose to chiseled turrets on the ridgetops and vultures circled lazily overhead. I meandered for hours through thickets of oak and massive contiguous stands of pure aspen whose leaves shimmered in the breeze with a sound like muffled applause. I sat and rested beneath ancient firs it would have taken three of me and my wingspan to encircle. Jays chattered and squawked in the canopy. Scat of various types dotted the trail. Muddy wallows showed where bears had recently rolled, and I held in my hands mule deer bones whose edges had been chamfered by the teeth of rodents. I put one such bone in my pocket, not really knowing why.

Back on the mountain, in the last of the day's light, we

tossed a Frisbee in the meadow below the tower. M.J. cooked dinner in an iron skillet, quesadillas with thick slices of avocado and fresh pico de gallo, heavy on jalapeños and fresh-squeezed lime. At dusk we lit kindling in the bonfire circle, downwind of the cabin, and stoked the fire with limbs gathered from the wooded edges of the meadow. We squatted on the periphery of the fire's warmth and sipped bourbon out of plastic cups.

After a couple of drinks, I told her of my time in Albuquerque and what I had learned there. She asked a number of questions, each of which I tried to answer. We spoke quietly. She came near and placed her arm around mine and held my left hand in hers, squeezing gently in the absence of words. For a long time we were silent, our eyes drawn to the mesmerizing leap and dance of the flames, friends joined in touch and tears.

What will you do now? she asked.

I told her I didn't know. I didn't think I could return to New York and pretend everything was unchanged, but the next move escaped me. I knew almost immediately that Emily's revelation had put an end to my desire to learn more about his life, at least any more than was locked away in my own memory. I couldn't bear to think there were other skeletons leering in the closet, waiting to be discovered, if only I managed to find the person with the knowledge of the secret. Perhaps there were no more secrets. One could hope.

Some of the speculations of those who had loved him had ultimately struck me as sound, or at least plausible. Depression, sure—my aunt Ruth had suspected as much, and she was about as close to him as anyone in the end. Anguish over the breakup with his girlfriend, okay. Been there myself, not good. But a secret he carried with him most of his life, a violation of the most brutal and sadistic sort? I couldn't wrap my mind around that one. I knew that was a cliché, but that was also it exactly: I couldn't absorb the thought, even as it leaped out as a probable cause. I couldn't fathom what had been done to him, how he'd lived with it, how it had changed him, what it had made him. I was already well aware that I hadn't known him the way a brother should. Now he slipped even further from reach—a failure of imagination on my part, a failure of empathy.

I knew this much: most of my prior assumptions had been called into doubt. Everything about him became infinitely more complicated. Cracks appeared in my story of who had failed him, and how, and when. The persistent notion that it was my inability to pick up the phone and call him that led to his death—my hold on that idea, already tenuous, became untenable. In the beginning, it had been as if I couldn't stand the thought that other factors contributed to his suicide, anything other than my failure to call him the day of it. I needed that distinction. I needed to believe I was that important to him. I had clung—far longer than a rational man would have—to the notion that my call would have been answered, and that it would have swayed him. In this way, it was never about him. It was always about me. The mind of the suicide survivor tends to be haunted by the thought that the dead passed judgment on the living, and that whatever else a suicide signifies, it can't help but contain the message that none of the living were enough of a sustaining connection to temper the allure of self-annihilation. The news that he was raped as a boy— this brought to the surface a series of hidden truths about his death, truths I had failed, somehow, to grasp. That it was, in the end, about no one but him; that it was nothing personal, at least insofar as his family was concerned. That perhaps there was nothing we could have done differently with the knowledge we possessed at the time. That he'd hidden his pain and shame so brilliantly, so capably—an acting job of unbelievable fortitude—that we never could have known him in all his complexity, no matter how hard we may have tried. No wonder he'd become a cipher in death. He'd been in hiding all his life.

Before I left her mountain, M.J. did me a favor I could never repay. She made noises about being bored in the lookout, wanting to get out on a fire, then maybe a camp crew for a hunting outfit—if only she could find a replacement on fire watch—but I suspect she secretly made it her mission to get me out of the city. She set it up as me doing her a favor, when in fact we both knew otherwise.

No one resists M.J.'s charms for long, and certainly not her boss back in district headquarters, to whom she took our plan devised by firelight and whiskey. Toby Cash Richards was born to that country, an aspiring logger turned schoolteacher and summer firefighter who'd worked his way up to become the Black Range district FMO (fire management officer) through the sheer ballsiness of letting things burn on landscape scale, in a landscape where fire was essential for a healthy forest. He was as country as country got. He knew his way around guns and was a master with a chain saw; he hunted elk with a bow and arrow, and people I came to trust eventually told me they never saw a man on a prescribed fire run drip torches with greater efficiency and zeal. If your truck was stuck in the mud or your horse had thrown you from the saddle, you wanted him alongside you. I once saw him drink a case of beer in the course of an afternoon and evening and wake the next morning at five o'clock to cook breakfast before another day in the woods, while the rest of us slumbered or moaned, at least until the smell of bacon roused us from our mummy bags. He did nothing half-assed, drinking included, and it never seemed to impinge on his capacity for work the next day, or his ability to two-step at closing time in the Pine Knot Bar.

After rehearsing her argument with me, M.J. got on the two-way radio and told Toby she needed out. She was going stir-crazy in her tower. She needed time on a crew in the woods, wanted to see the action from another angle, up close and personal on the hot, smoky edges of a fire. She told him I needed a career change and some time to think, that I was competent with maps and binoculars, and that she'd personally train me in all the idiosyncrasies of the lookout's tools—a ten-minute job, she said, and he laughed. She talked like a raving pyromaniac, sick of looking at fire from a distance. She knew her audience. Toby, I would learn, was nothing if not keen on fire. He respected her gumption. Eventually he buckled, said fine, he'd take a chance on a greenhorn, and when could I be back and ready for duty?

Fifteen days, it was decided. I'd offer two weeks' notice at the paper and take the earliest Saturday flight back. I'd relieve M.J. for whatever remained of the season, no guarantees on the length of my employment, rainfall and fire danger the deciding factors.

After she'd signed off the radio, M.J. stared at me with as serious a look as she could muster.

Don't screw this up, she said.

I told her I was so grateful I would do whatever it took to earn her trust in me.

Her face contorted in laughter.

Kidding! she howled. It's not possible to screw up as a lookout, as long as you stay awake on the job.

I gave her a bear hug and shouldered my pack, took one last long look around the mountain I would soon call home. On my way down the trail I built a cairn on a wind-whipped ridge, in a place I felt sure no one but me would ever visit—a place as wild as the feeling in my heart—and set the deer bone inside of it.

I met Paul Gigot as I got off the elevator on my second-to-last day of work at the *Journal.*

Well, it's been a pleasure, I said.

Yes, good luck, he said.

Now you'll be able to hire someone who's more enthusiastic about working on the editorial page, I said.

We've had a change of plans, he said. Your replacement is only going to work on Leisure & Arts.

He stepped onto the elevator and threw me a little half wave, half salute.

I'd always expected I would one day be shown the door. It was some kind of miracle that I'd lasted as long as I had. Having earned my original position at the paper by means of sanitizing the truth to my advantage, I had to admire the fact that I'd been purged by my own hand. But what was I going to do about it? Rescind my resignation? Beg him to let me stay?

So long, I said, waving.

Watching over the wilderness of the Gila country, alone with the wind and the stars and the bears and the birds, day after day, night after night—eventually season after season, for more than a decade—was far from easy at first. The enforced solitude made me not just mentally but physically uncomfortable, like a snake molting its skin. All the stimulations and diversions on which I'd come to rely in the city were gone, except the whiskey I made sure to pack in on mules, with all my other supplies. Beyond that I had only myself and the landscape, nothing but time and nothing to do but watch. At long last I had a way of being in the world that didn't feel fraudulent.

Outside was a world that dwarfed the self, and I fell hard for the country, especially those parts of it that remained wildest. The headwaters of the Gila River encompassed the first place on earth where an industrial society made a conscious decision to avoid disturbing the landscape with motorized or mechanized machines, an administrative order of the Forest Service in 1924, and it remained a harsh and forbidding landscape, unpunctured by roads, where all travel occurred by foot or by horse. Day by day the place worked its magic on me. Its harshness spoke to something harsh inside of me. Its cruelty attracted. And it was beautiful as only those pieces of the old, wild world can be, places where the ancient music of birdsong and elk bugle still plays undrowned by man and his tools. I lost myself in the manic profusion of starlight, the blinding glare of noon; I hovered in numinous mysteries, laughed like a madman at my unexpected good fortune. By staying put through all the various moods and weathers I couldn't help but feel awe of a sort I'd previously thought unattainable, an ecstatic dissolution of the self. The place tore me down and remade me; its indifference to my cares and sorrows was magisterial and, in unexpected ways, comforting. I had believed that the streets of New York were the pinnacle of indifference to the individual human life and I had been mistaken. In the streets of New York you could always perform and at least pretend someone watched, or recede yourself into the act of watching, a necessary member of the audience for the performance all around you. Alone on a mountain there were no such luxuries.

Having seen two towers reduced to a crumble of rubble on fire, I couldn't help but appreciate the poetic reversal of watching for fires from a tower in the wilderness. It felt like a useful act of witness, like journalism minus the obsession with ephemera. But it's also the case that in my renewed grief for Dan and all that he had suffered, I wanted to honor the gift he'd given me the last time I saw him, the gift of an incomparable view of mountains and desert from above the great rift valley of the Rio Grande. From the moment I stepped foot inside the seven-by-seven-foot cab of M.J.'s tower I was reminded of the basket of Dan's balloon, and the unimpeded view from her peak—a view that included the great rift valley of the Rio Grande—called back that long-ago feeling of flight, the dignity and grandeur of floating eye-level with distant mountains. I wanted to perpetuate that feeling. I wanted to live inside of it again, remaining close to what was best in him. If it took an act of intentional downward mobility to do so, trading a job in journalism for a vocation less than a quarter as remunerative, so be it. That great sweep of sky more than made up the difference. The adventure he had dreamed of but never attempted, soaring over the Sandias in a big wind—I could live a version of it every day, afternoons amid the lightning, mornings above the clouds.

I never really left southern New Mexico after that first taste, not in my heart of hearts anyway, although it would take me another two years before I left the city for good. While there during those last dismal winters between fire seasons, I mimicked a human being with cosmopolitan cares but I no longer had any such thing, if indeed I ever had. The first winter I burned through my Dow Jones 401(k) and looked in vain for freelance work; I participated in the big anti-war protest, when half a million people took to the streets to issue a warning on the rush to invade Iraq on ginned-up pretenses. I'd always thought of the city as the natural home of free speech and collective action but I watched while pro-testers were penned in like hamsters by metal barricades and threatened with arrest on the flimsiest of pretexts. Innocent people were brutally cuffed and stuffed, and cops on horseback charged crowds for no good reason, threaten-ing the safety of parents and the kids they carried on their shoulders. Those of us who lived in the city that suffered the brunt of the terrorist attack made clear our distaste for visiting a misguided version of the devastation on Baghdad, and we were treated like dogs, some of us manhandled and jailed, all of us told to shut up and keep shopping and the wise men in Washington would handle the rest. Marching felt like pissing into a headwind. The storm was coming, and we knew it. Chicken hawks were in charge, itching for glory. But someone had to say no, even if—especially if—those in power viewed us with contempt.

In the bitter last days I worked a series of demoraliz-ing jobs, dreaming of the next fire season, the low point arriving when I signed on at twelve bucks an hour to tran-scribe tapes of CEOs and senior executives shilling for their companies to something called the *Wall Street Transcript*, which published the interviews verbatim and at preposter-ous length in a weekly printed booklet. And by tapes I do mean tapes. I played the cassettes with a foot pedal that allowed me to stop the recording or rewind when necessary. I'd have preferred not to suffer such humiliation, but I had to make a living somehow, and the *WST* was the only thing I could find.

At the end of my first fire season I flew to Minneapolis and rented a car for the drive to the little town in southern Minnesota where my parents lived. On the day I was to leave to catch a flight to New York, when they were both home from work for their lunch hour, I asked them to sit with me at the kitchen table. I said I was very sorry for what I was about to tell them but I thought they deserved to know.

My father's reaction was about what I expected: unemotional, rational in the extreme. That explains some things, he said, when I finished telling him what Emily had told me. I asked him what it explained, not because I didn't feel similarly—victims of childhood sexual abuse are many times more likely to attempt suicide than the general population, for starters—but because I was curious about his take. He said that he'd always suspected Dan of being afraid of sexual intimacy. He'd had so few girlfriends in his life, and when he lost them he was disconsolate in a way that was hard to fathom. Nonetheless, the loss of Wendy, the proximate cause of his suicide, had never seemed a sufficient reason for putting a gun to his head. The fact that he'd carried with him such a secret for most of his life placed his difficulties with women in a new light.

Do you know who it was? he asked.

When I offered a name, his jaw set in resignation tinged with anger.

I can't say that surprises me, he said.

My mother reacted about as I'd expected too. Her face suddenly drained of color; she wept a few silent tears while my father and I speculated about what it all meant, and then she went to their bedroom and closed the door.

Just before I left to catch a flight home from Minneapolis, my mother reemerged and said to me, There's a blue notebook in the office, on top of a box in the closet. You can read it if you want.

After she and my father left again for work, I found the notebook and sat at the kitchen table.

June 3rd—I was at work & Bill told me that Bob had called & said to go home for a minute. I thought he'd hurt his back. When I walked in the door, Bob was leaning against the kitchen sink with Father Evers beside him. Bob grabbed me and pulled me against him. I thought he said Dad died, then I realized he said Dan. I was stunned. After a short length of time, sitting on the couch, I asked Father Evers if Dan would go to hell for this—I didn't know if Dan believed in God. After that I don't remember much for the next week. My heavy heart was in my throat & I couldn't swallow or breathe. I couldn't eat, drink, think, or sleep. The neighbor kid asked his dad why we were having so much fun if Dan had died. He had heard all of these people out on the deck all night long, laughing and telling stories, trying to deal with his death in the best way they knew how.

Sam & Jan went to Granite Falls to tell Lisa & bring her home. Who told Phil about Dan? When did he find out? Was he alone when he heard? How terrible that he had to take that long plane ride by himself.

Dan called Sunday at noon. Thinking back on that conversation, I think he knew what he was going to do. He said he and Wendy were having trouble. I said, "Give her some time." He said, "Oh I'll give her a lot of time." If I had only known, I would have got on a plane right then & gone down to see him. I forgot to tell him "I love you" before I handed the phone to Bob so they could talk about fishing.

Sam & Jan helped us through the funeral decisions. We were told to bring friends in case we couldn't understand any of the decisions we needed to make. I'm sure that Mr. Almlie thought we would be VERY distressed over this suicide. Lisa was with us & helped make some of the decisions, which I hardly remember. I only knew I didn't want to bury him, I wanted him alive.

Bob made the decision not to see his body, after Almlie said it wouldn't be a good idea. I regret that decision to this day, but don't hold it against Bob. He wanted to remember him like he was, not with a hole blown through his head—

maybe he didn't have his face left? We were glad when Lisa went to the funeral home late the next night when his body finally came in. She came back reporting that he looked fine. She only saw, under the cloth on his face, a bruised looking spot on the one side, & they had his eyes sewn shut. She cut off a small lock of his hair & she brought it back to me. That's all I have left of him. I keep it in a small coin purse in a drawer. I can't bring it out to look at because it brings all the heartache back again.

It takes all my strength to not think about him & talk about him. That's the only way I've been able to get through these past 5 yrs.

Even writing this, the tears are flowing so hard I can hardly see the page.

Every year on this day, and on his birthday, I just want to stay in bed. I don't want to do anything or see anybody. Thank God today fell on Sunday so I didn't have to go to work.

Were we bad parents that we didn't raise our son to feel strong enough not to take his own life?

Now when I see a beautiful morning, a beautiful sunset, a bird, lovers in a park, people fishing, I think: Why did he want to give that up? Why did he want to deprive us of his birthdays, his wedding, his children, visits to his home?

I need someone to say the right words to me so that I can deal with this heartbreaking sadness in a positive way because right now—all I do is cry.

I worry about my kids being lonely and being alone.

There are days when I feel guilty for not crying or for being able to sleep.

Double rainbow on his funeral day.

Liberated by writing this down.

When asked how many kids I have, it's hard to answer three. I'm afraid they'll ask me about Dan. And if I talk about him, I'll cry.

It's my birthday today, Phil called and we talked for 2 hours, some about Dan. I cry while I'm talking but it still feels good to talk.

When I hear a song on the radio that I knew he liked I want to turn it off—but I can't force myself. If it stays on maybe he is close by listening.

I copied this down, word for word, transcribing through my own tears, and then I returned the notebook to the place where I'd found it, unaware I'd begun writing this book.

Until then my thoughts on my brother's death remained very rarely spoken aloud, mostly locked up in private note-books—tens of thousands of words' worth of the most bleak and lugubrious maunderings—but my mother's brave act of connection set me free. If she could share her innermost thoughts, maybe I could a tell a story worth sharing too, in my own rude way.

Shortly afterward she sent me a package containing VHS tapes of Dan's varsity wrestling matches. She didn't think she would ever be able to watch them, so she wanted me to have them, just in case. I'd become the documentar-ian in the family, the keeper of my brother's records—pho-tographs, report cards, test score results, 4-H ribbons, bank statements, wrestling tourney programs, balloon pilot logs—which I saved with the usual journalist's pack-rat mentality, except in this case it had all added up to squat in answer to the major question. I tried twice to watch him but I couldn't get more than a few minutes in. He was as I remembered, fun to watch, tough in the clinch, a technical master and an escape artist more than a brute force. The incongruity of seeing him alive, grappling his opponents into submis-sion—he won twenty-five matches his senior year—was too much for me.

I was surprised that my father wouldn't wish to keep the tapes, but then I remembered that more than once over the previous years he'd told me that he refused to dwell in the past, that he would not let his son's death define his life. I have no reason to doubt that he succeeded through a herculean effort of will, or maybe just a cold shrug of contempt for unpleasantness of any sort. I know for a fact that he thought my interest in the story to be an unhealthy wallowing in darkness—his alien, oversensitive son, gripped by morbid curiosities. His of all the theories I'd heard rang truest, that whatever sickness festered inside his youngest son, the suicidal impulse had been just that, an impulse he mistakenly heeded with the aid of booze and a gun, that all too lethal combination for sad young men. I had the presence of mind to avoid telling my father that I felt certain, almost from the moment I heard the news, that my brother's death would be the most interesting thing to happen in what remained of my life, that surpassing it in sheer riveting power would take something so horrible as to be unimaginable, or so wonderful as to be unreal, and that to deny these facts would have taken more determination than I possessed. My father went his way, I went mine, and never the twain shall meet, though I'm closer to him now in other ways than I've ever been.

Later on, a little bit braver, or maybe merely masochistic, I stuck a tape recorder under both my parents' noses, one at a time in private moments, conducting what I called *research*, and what came out of it was totally unexpected, some of it funny, some of it sad, most of it wildly off topic. I couldn't make myself make them talk about it for longer than a question or two, and they weren't prepared to go there on their own. To speak of it with my mother, in particular, seemed a willful act of torture. I had received a very targeted education in the art of making people talk about uncomfortable things, and still I couldn't do it, not to them.

They'd overcome too much. My father had transformed himself from failed farmer to bank vice president; they traveled now, drank nice wine, cultivated a beautiful garden, had a whole new set of late-life friends. How could I justify continuing to poke at the wound? "All families of suicides are alike," Janet Malcolm has written. "They wear a kind of permanent letter S on their chests. Their guilt is never assuaged. Their anxiety never lifts. They are freaks among families the way prodigies are freaks among individuals." That about sums it up, except for the prodigy comparison. By definition, prodigies are blessed with a gift. The families of suicides are not blessed.

In the winter of 2002 I undertook a journey I'd been planning and dreading for months, all the while in silence. I knew well my capacity for anger; I knew, in other words, that I had needed some time to chill. Plan some lines of inquiry. Judge what it was I wanted to know. But since I doubted I'd extract a confession, it was less about what I wanted to know and more about what I wanted *him* to know. Maybe one shred of justice could be wrung from the whole sad affair. He would forever know that I knew.

So I traveled out of my way to see him, in a town better left unnamed. I found him at his workplace—a little flabbier than I remembered him, a bit too falsely jovial, in the manner of an upbeat high school football coach. I hadn't called ahead to apprise him of my visit. He appeared to be baffled by my coming but he shook my hand, invited me up to his office. I sensed immediately the pride he felt in having an office.

A dear connection of his had died not long before, a woman I had cause to know in my youth, and I used this as the pretext for dropping by. I told him that personal business had brought me to the vicinity, and since I'd found myself with spare time on my hands, I wanted to offer my condolences in person.

He told me about the woman's final hours, some touching last moments they'd shared, a death with ease and dignity. I nodded my head at all the right moments. He asked about my life in New York. I told him it had been good but was coming to an end. I'd quit my job in journalism. I had no prospects there anymore. I was broke. My candor clearly made him uneasy. People didn't talk this way where we were from.

Our conversation dwindled to inanities. The moment had arrived to announce my true purpose. I had fantasized about announcing it with a roundhouse to his nose; now that I found myself within arm's reach of him I felt nervous, even ashamed somehow. I could barely bring myself to look at him. In fact I turned away, looked at the wall. What if I was wrong? What if I had the wrong guy? Or worse, what if my brother had made up a story for sympathy in a moment of vulnerability, when he felt himself to be losing his fiancée? Horrified that I would attribute to my brother such conniving instincts, I forgot the question I'd rehearsed. I nearly rose and left without explanation. Then it returned to me.

You're a God-fearing man, correct? I said.

He appeared mystified. I go to church, yes, if that's what you mean.

Have you asked God's forgiveness for what you did to my brother?

There was a pause. He asked me what I meant, so I told him.

I have no recollection of any such thing, he said.

I pressed the point. He became flustered, sweaty, red of face, but still he denied it. Tellingly, I thought, he never denied doing it; he denied any memory of having done it. I have no recollection of such a thing, he said, over and over. We went around and around, and his story never changed. I didn't have a leg to stand on—a secondhand piece of news, a rumor whispered from the lips of the dead. There existed no corroborating witness, no one to offer incriminating testimony. I knew it was folly to believe that he'd confess if I persisted in my questioning. Maybe he'd truly convinced himself it hadn't happened, a strategic lapse of memory that allowed him to avoid succumbing to a crippling guilt. Maybe he really hadn't done it, and I was crudely bullying an innocent man in an effort to make myself feel like a soldier in the cause of justice, as if our confrontation could possibly balance the scales. I would never know for sure. I could only trust my gut, and my gut told me to pray there had been no other victims, as if prayer could make it so.

I gave him a scrap of paper with my phone number on it, told him to call me if his recollection changed.

Before I left I wished him good luck with his god.

I knew I'd never hear from him.

Try though I might, I could think of nothing more to do with this bit of innuendo, not without inviting a lawsuit for slander. It was a bitter and unsatisfying coda to a story I sometimes thought I'd rather not have unearthed—a story that, despite appearing to offer a perverse absolution to Dan and those of us who loved him, still had about it the odor of a spoiled fruit.

In the coming years I would often think of Wendy, Dan's last girlfriend, wondering what had become of her. Though I asked around, no one knew how to reach her. No one had seen her since the memorial service in Albuquerque a few weeks after his death. No one even remembered her last name.

Eventually it occurred to me to look more closely at Dan's balloon pilot log, in which he'd recorded the date and time of his flights, their duration, his launch and landing sites, plus any passengers he'd had on board. For years it had sat unopened in a box I carted with me every time I moved, a box marked ALL THINGS DAN, into which I'd tossed it after a cursory look at its first few pages. She was there, of course. Along with her two children, she'd been a frequent companion on those flights over the last eight months of his life.

Though I now knew her full name, I took it no further. Another year passed, then two, and still I resisted the urge to track her down. I knew some of what she'd been through and I feared my phone call would be greeted as an unwelcome reminder of an episode she'd rather forget.

There were those among our family and friends who'd blamed her for Dan's death. It had come so soon after their breakup that the impulse was understandable. By this reckoning, she'd carelessly played with his heart; she'd had her fun with a younger man, used him as a plaything, a distraction from the pain of her marital split, and when the novelty had worn off she'd dumped him. Had these speculations ever reached her ears? I hoped not. Had she intuited them nonetheless? Perhaps. The thought of it made me sick— her having to reckon with that sort of guilt. I'd never been seduced by the temptation to blame her. People break up all the time. A certain amount of pain and sadness ensues, but to kill oneself over it seemed to me an act so extreme and vengeful, so blindly self-regarding, as to be monstrous. Despite having tested the idea, I ultimately couldn't believe my brother to be that sort of monster.

One night I typed her name in a search engine and found she still lived in New Mexico. I called information and procured a number, which I wrote on a scrap of paper and tucked in my wallet. I carried it around for months. As more and more time went by, it seemed less and less likely that I would ever muster the nerve to call. I didn't know what I could say to her; I couldn't imagine what she'd say to me. We'd never met. We'd never spoken a word. I'd come across one snapshot of the two of them, in a collection of photos kept by my mother: she was thin and pretty, with blond hair and green eyes, and they were sitting next to each other, turned toward someone out of the frame, both of them laughing, two beers on the table in front of them. I often looked at this photo and tried to imagine what unforeseen trajectory her life had taken in the aftermath of the bullet. I wasn't sure I wanted to know the truth. In some matters the truth, when we find it, is worse than our worst imaginings.

After a couple of glasses of whiskey one evening—sixteen years, nine months, and two days after his death—I decided to hell with it. Maybe she'd hate me for calling, maybe not, but there was only one way to find out. I dialed the number. She picked up on the third ring. I told her my name, who I was. She said, Oh, okay, and waited in silence for what would come next.

I said there was one thing I needed to tell her, one thing I felt sure Dan would want me to say on his behalf if he knew we were speaking: I'm sorry.

I waited in silence for what would come next. I figured fifty-fifty she'd tell me off and hang up.

Thank you, she said.

My call was unexpected, to say the least. So much time had passed, and she hadn't seen or heard from a soul who'd known him since very shortly after his death, though she still thought of him all the time. She remembered him as a very private person, very quiet, but generally happy, smart for his age, good at his job, a skillful balloon pilot, a take-charge kind of guy. His self-confidence was very attractive. When he showed up it was as if a ray of sunshine had come bursting into her life. He'd made her life better during a difficult time. She told me he'd been mature for his age, she'd been immature for hers, and they'd met in the sweet spot in the middle.

They'd spent almost every minute together when he

wasn't working, shared dinner together every night, went out often, usually to a bar in Rio Rancho, a suburb of Albuquerque. They drank and played darts, hung out with friends. They were having fun, smitten with each other's company, and they indulged—perhaps a little too much, she admitted. He'd lost a fiancée, she'd lost a husband, but they'd found each other, and for a while it felt like he was everything she needed.

He'd melded well with her kids. They liked and respected him. In fact they still talked about him sometimes, all these years later. At the time, though, it was complicated. Her life had felt tangled, too many things unresolved. She and her husband were fighting over custody, over the division of property. The kids thought Dan might be the cause of their parents' breakup. He talked to them honestly, told them he wasn't there to replace their father but was open to listening and helping in any way he could. You have to get back in touch with them, she remembered him telling her. They're hurting. They need you.

She took his words to heart. She decided she needed a break, mostly for the sake of her children. They agreed to put things on hold and revisit their situation when everything cooled down. They both knew this was for the best, though it wasn't an easy decision.

That same weekend he moved back into his apartment. It was his first time alone there in months; he'd been living with her since not long after they'd met.

He left on a Friday night. By sometime late Sunday he was dead.

It was the strangest thing, she said, but that night I swore I heard his truck drive past. I asked my daughter, Did you hear Dan's truck just now? Mom, you're hearing things, she told me. Don't be silly.

She could still smell and taste things from the day she got the news. First his boss had called and asked if Dan was with her, since no one had heard from him. She said no, they'd had a difficult weekend, talking bad to each other after the split. He'd been drunk when last they spoke. She could only assume he was sleeping off a hangover.

It made us all feel so empty, she said, so sickly sad given all he'd accomplished and all he still had ahead of him. It just didn't make sense. I tried to come up with an explanation. Was it work stress that left him feeling overwhelmed? Was it depression I hadn't noticed? Was the breakup the final straw? And if so, how dare he?

She evaded the temptation to assign herself guilt: it was his choice, after all. Besides sadness and shock, she felt anger—a tremendous, devouring anger. He'd had so many friends. He could have reached out to one of them. He had other options. Instead he took the one that could not be undone, a permanent solution to a temporary problem.

That was a turning point in her life, as it would have to be. Afterward, she lost her taste for drinking. The bar they'd hung out in, their special place, closed, and she was glad to see it gone. She couldn't have gone there without him. It would have been too painful.

She'd never remarried. Her kids had become the focus of her life, in addition to the small business she ran. Her son was a property manager and lived in Seattle. Her daughter lived nearby in New Mexico and had two little kids of her own. She'd never imagined herself a grandma, but now here she was.

I have these déjà vu moments, she said. They bring on a memory and it's like he's here again, like he never left. Whenever I notice a hot air balloon, which is pretty often in Albuquerque, I think of him, or when I visit the post office and see the security cameras he installed. They're still there. I guess I shouldn't be surprised that they'd last. He was so good at everything he did.

We spoke for a bit about ourselves, our work. I wasn't sure if I should bring the conversation back around to Dan or just let it go. It felt a little unfair to allude to the possibility that he'd been raped—as if this fact might color her memory of him—but it felt even more unfair not to.

She was shocked to hear it. He'd never said anything about it to her, and she'd never suspected such a thing. She didn't know what to make of it. She'd need some time to think on it.

I told her I hadn't called her looking for theories or answers; I had all the answers I would ever have, and they would always remain not enough. I'd called her only to connect, one person to another, over the memory of someone we'd both loved.

He was a wonderful man, she said.

I know, I said.

I try not to define our time together by how his life ended. It's hard. But I think I've managed it.

I'm glad of that, I said. And I'm glad to have heard someone speak so sweetly of the man he was. I haven't had that chance very often.

She accepted my offer to meet for dinner if ever I was in her neck of the woods. It would be nice, we both agreed, to sit down someday, face-to-face, now that a silence had been broken.

When in the course of conversation the subject of siblings arises, I've been known to fudge the truth and leave off mention of Dan—heeding the old taboo. I have a sister, I say. She's a joy to be around, with a ribald sense of humor and a skeptical intelligence. I picked on her mercilessly as a child, but she forgave me for it, even later laughed about it with me. She left home at the age of seventeen, moved in with a boyfriend, attained a GED, worked all sorts of jobs, including, like me, night baker. She's now a corrections officer in Minnesota, a Harley rider, a lover of camping in the north country in the summertime. She tells fascinating stories about her work in a medium-security state pen, the damaged men, the ethnic gangs, the squalor and the silliness, the desperation. She lives in a little burg of six hundred people, in an immaculately kept house filled with books and cozy places to sit, on the last street in town, where the howling of the winter wind across the open prairie gives her a healthy appreciation for the adversities of life, as if she needed that. Twice divorced, she's had unfortunate luck with men but never betrayed a worry over her own self-sufficiency. She's well schooled in the tactics of restraint, even teaches others in her line of work. I know damn well she could hurt me if she needed to. I love her no less for the fact that I talk to her on the phone maybe four or five times a year, maximum. When we do talk, we tell each other the truth unvarnished. We understand we owe each other that much.

I told her once how on the day of Dan's funeral I spoke with one of his good friends, a fellow farm kid, who told me that back in high school he and Dan would drive out to the farm on summer nights and sit in the yard drinking beer, listening to the crickets in the fields. No matter where their evening had taken them it always ended at the farm. They'd park in the lane and sit on the tailgate of Dan's truck, looking up at the stars. We'd been gone for several years by then, and bit by bit the place was coming undone, first the windows of the house shot out, then chunks of good lumber wrenched free and hauled off, finally whole walls smashed and copper wire stripped. Each time they went back the place looked worse.

It pissed him off, John said. He used to hope we'd find the vandals there when we showed up, so we could catch them in the act and whip their asses.

The worse the place looked, the more Dan talked about the way it was when we were kids. Dan could tell stories for hours, apparently, about us playing kick-the-can with our cousins from Iowa, the way we slid down the stairs in the house inside our sleeping bags, pretending to be bobsledders, or the snow forts we built in the woods behind the chicken coop.

He loved that place, John said. He hated having to leave it. I'm just glad he was gone for New Mexico by the time it burned down.

While he lived I'd never thought to wonder whether he had the same nostalgic yearnings I did, whether he, like me, drove there in later years and walked through the shell of what was once our life. It saddened me to think we had this in common and never knew it, even worse to think it took his death for me to learn it. We'd been told so often we had nothing in common that we came to believe it; this was the first of our misunderstandings, though hardly the last. Unlike me, he never tried to bleed the country boy out of himself, drop by solitary drop. There had been a time in my adolescence when I began to view our failure at farming as a blessing of sorts. It untethered me from a family calling passed down the generations, set me free to make of myself whatever I could dream up—the American way and the way I preferred it. If given the chance, Lisa and I agreed, he'd never have left.

When I went back to the farm—rarely, always alone—I was looking for some piece of myself I had lost in a place whose loss, paradoxically, had liberated me to become my true self. Maybe my hunch about him was wrong, and he went back not because he'd lost something of himself but because he wanted close contact with something he would always have or always be. We each eventually drifted away to distant cities, but I was the restless striver, the chameleon, trying on a series of potential identities, while he became a slightly different version of what he'd always been, a shitkickin' country boy who adopted a northern finger of the Chihuahuan Desert as his new home country, though not for long.

Because our leaving the farm marked a kind of rupture in our lives, I return in memory to the time before, years I'm tempted to think of as prelapsarian. The memories are vague, though, and faded like the color in the Polaroids my mother saves in photo albums, but in spite of their haziness they're a major part of what I turn to when I try to reconstitute the brothers we once were.

Much of what I recall arises from pure sense memory. The heavy feel of bottle glass in our hands, empty pints and quarts of booze the previous farmer, Old Man Leysen, hid everywhere in the grove of woods behind the house where Dan and I played in summertime. The scaly texture of the wild asparagus we picked outside the barbed-wire fence on the northwest corner of the pasture for our mother to cook with dinner. The milky surface of the ponds in the low spots of the pasture, where we played broom ball in winter, bruising our knees on the ice. The neat cords of firewood we stacked next to the house after our father split the rounds he'd bucked up with his chain saw by the river. The seed-dust smell of the granary where we laid traps for mice. The crunch of shells as we walked through ancient lake beds drained for farmland, picking rocks. The dirt beneath our fingernails from our practice farming in the side yard. That beautiful soil that crumbled in our hands and smelled of ten thousand years of prairie fecundity. All of this I suspected Dan remembered too, the shared geography of a vanished way of life, though we never spoke of it.

Sometimes after a hard summer rain we'd step into the yard with a flashlight and a pail and collect the elongated earthworms stretched in the wet grass, dozens and dozens of them writhing in the dark. They contracted as soon as they were touched, and they left a film on our hands when we handled them. No bait was more effective in catching bull-heads. They were so fat you could pinch them in half and bait two hooks with one worm. Fishing was our major pastime away from farm work; if we left the farm it was usually to buy groceries in town, attend church on Sunday, or ride our bikes to the bridge across the river with our poles and tackle boxes. Those hours were the sweetest of my childhood, brothers at play on the land, at play on the water, a simple enjoyment of each other's presence amid the thrill of catching fish.

There was an old schoolhouse just down the road—an abandoned one-room country school with a potbellied stove and a blackboard still hung on one wall. Our grandmother received her first years of education there, in the depths of the Depression. When we played inside of it, often with Lisa alongside us, dust motes stirred in the light slanting through the cracked windowpanes. One day the three of us startled a skunk who'd been taking shelter under the floor-boards. We ran when we saw it, and it ran when it saw us, and thankfully a moving target isn't easy to hit when the thing taking aim is moving too. We'd heard that the only way to rid yourself of the stench of a skunk was to take a bath in tomato juice, a thought that repulsed us and, mercifully, a remedy we never had to endure. One close call was enough. We never played in the old schoolhouse again. A short while later it was struck by lightning and charred. Someone decided the risk of it burning was too great—it was only a short distance from a telephone pole whose wires passed close overhead—so it was demolished, the wood hauled away for kindling in someone's stove, a harbinger of what was to come for our own home.

When I picture us a little later, around the ages of nine and ten, I see myself with a basketball shooting endlessly at the hoop on the side of the granary, and I see Dan hunched over some project in a corner of the garage, which was actually a kind of workshop. It was a world of metallic smells and funky fumes that made you feel funny if you sniffed them deeply at close range, but all the various tools nestled in boxes or hung on nails seemed to speak to him of a world that made sense, a world you could take apart and reassemble with your hands, a world in which every thing fit with some other thing and if it stopped fitting you either fixed it or threw it out and replaced it with another. It was a world he felt drawn to by skill and temperament. It was a world he in fact mastered, working with his hands all his short life. A car engine was a world to be taken apart and rebuilt. A china cabinet was a world to be carved from nature and assembled as functional art. His pieces, if you knew when he'd made them, showed evidence of his ever-increasing skill. They were scattered in homes from the Midwest to the Southwest and places between. I have seen and touched them. Everything fits. Everything is smooth and plumb and buffed to a sheen. It seems only natural to wonder if his undoing was that thing he could not make fit in the story of himself, the one thing that did not make sense and could never be fixed or discarded.

Whenever I'm in Minnesota I visit his grave, but its chilly rectitude, the cold headstone, do not summon him. There he's simply underground inside a box. I visit too our old home on the farm, but the architecture of the place, the house and barns in which we lived and worked together, are nothing but a ghostly memory. Maybe our erasure from the land erased my memory, more so than his death; either way, what I've written here is most of what I have in the way of story from my childhood. I wish there were more. Maybe it will come in old age, as some say it does. For now, when I want to be close to him, I visit that cairn I built on a lonely ridge of the Black Range. Over the years I've added more chamfered bones, antlers and potsherds and turquoise beads, snake skins and mushrooms, turkey feathers, stones, the serendipitous accumulations of my evening walks. He'd like it there, I feel certain. The view from the ridge is wild as all get-out, the deep headwaters canyons of a trout stream to the west, the distant valley of the Rio Grande across the desert to the east. It's as wild a place as you can still find in the Lower 48.

In the summer of my twelfth year on the mountain it

burned, as we'd all known it would one day. I watched as the plume took off in a running crown fire of two-hundred-foot flames, the smoke billowing black into the sky, as if roaring from a fissure in the basement of the world. A helicopter plucked me from the mountain ahead of the flames. I watched the spectacle for a month from a different tower thirty miles north. The fire covered two hundred square miles in the end. On the hottest day of its run it torched ten thousand acres in an afternoon. The smoke plume rose into the lower troposphere, a pulsing column of heat topped by its own pyrocumulus cloud, from which could be heard the rumble of thunder. Charred oak leaves fluttered to the ground as far away as twenty-five miles.

I returned after the late-summer rains. It was a peculiar hike in, the first time back. The burn area was still closed to the public, so I let myself through a locked gate on the highway near the forest boundary, aware that the country was entirely mine, for a little while anyway. As I walked and gawked I added everything I saw to my memory's palimpsest of the landscape, the original layer as I'd found it in the beginning with M.J., another layer as I'd seen it before a fir-beetle outbreak killed thousands of trees, and another layer after, one from the whirlybird on my way out, and now the newest and most radical revision as it greeted me in the aftermath of the burn, black as black gets in places. About two-thirds of the way to the top, big islands of untouched forest appeared where the fire'd had no impact on the canopy. From the open meadow on top you couldn't tell there'd been a fire at all. The peak still wore a cap of green, the grass luxuriant from the rains, the trees along the peak's edges untouched. I wandered around looking for the places where the fire's fingers made their highest runs. I didn't have to go far. A couple hundred yards in any direction there were big patches of scorched earth. Back on top, an hour after my arrival, something bright green quivered in the grass between the cabin and the outhouse: a tree frog. In all my seasons there I'd never seen one. It felt like an omen, a sign that despite the tremendous changes, the life of the mountain carried on as before.

The next day I visited the cairn with the half-charred pelvis of a mule deer. I wasn't sure what I'd find. All around stood the spooky pikes of burnt trees, a forest poised between what it had been and what it would be. Ash had turned to mud on the ground. No birds sang, but the grass was already greening, the oaks resprouting; soon the birds would return, the aspens would burst from the char, the cycle of death and rebirth gone around once more. Strangely, the landscape felt more like home than ever. Perhaps when your childhood home is lost to the bankers and then lost forever when its new owner torches everything on the property for two more acres of tillable land, you can't help but be mesmerized by the erasures achieved by fire. Perhaps when your brother ends his life with a bullet to the brain, you can't help but feel an intuitive understanding of the forces of earthly destruction. Standing inside the black can feel like a form of belonging.

By some miracle the cairn remained untouched by the flames, solid as the day I'd built it, a tiny oasis amid the burn scar. I removed the cap rock. I placed the bone inside. I felt the enormity of his loss once more. The pain of it never does fade entirely, never will—no doubt it disfigured me in ways that will endure for what remains of my life—but at last I found a place to put it where it wouldn't eat me alive. My devotion to his memory led me there, the place I venerate above all others on earth, my little voodoo shrine to the lost and the damned, as wild and remote as the country of grief itself.